A LIFE WORTH LIVING

A LIFE WORTH LIVING

*Finding Your Purpose and Daring to
Live the Life You've Imagined*

KEVIN JOHN DELANEY

STONE CASTLE
—PUBLISHING—

Published by Stone Castle Publishing. Printed in the United States of America.

ISBN 978-1-7354052-0-9

ISBN 978-1-7354052-1-6 (eBook)

For Aidan, Brendan, Kylie, and Vicky.
You make mine a life worth living.

Life is either a daring adventure or nothing at all.

— HELEN KELLER

CONTENTS

INTRODUCTION

My Story

Eleven years, nine months, and twenty-three days ago doctors said I had twenty-four hours to live. I wasn't listening because I was in a coma, my body failing fast. The doctors were talking with my family, and everyone had more questions than answers.

Several days earlier, I had asked my doctor if I was going to die, and he told me the chances were high that I would not survive. I was forty-two years old, active and healthy, and all I could think about were the many things in life I still wanted to do. First on the list was seeing my three kids grow up.

It was May 2008, and I was in the hospital. Again. I had been there the day before for an outpatient surgery, a simple procedure to remove my gallbladder. I was in and out of surgery and released from the hospital within a few hours to recover at home. That night, my fever spiked, and I returned to the hospital to find out why. I stayed overnight for observation, and by morning I knew something serious was happening, different from anything I'd experienced before.

The journey started six months earlier. It was a Monday morning in October, and I was in the kitchen getting ready for work. Without warning, everything went black, and I collapsed unconscious on the floor. I remained there, slumped against the cabinets until paramedics revived me. I would spend the next six months navigating one health crisis after another, in what would be the most challenging time in my life.

To determine what caused my blackout, I went through a barrage of tests. I had blood tests, ECGs, and echocardiograms. I wore a heart monitor, ran treadmill tests, and had PET scans. In December, I had a tilt table test that put me into cardiac arrest. Twice. A nurse performed CPR, and I woke up looking into the faces of my panicked doctors. My "severe clinical reaction" was not what they were expecting.

Before I knew it, I was rolling down the hospital hallways on my way to the operating room. I had vasovagal syncope, a condition where my heart rate and blood pressure sometimes drop suddenly, reducing blood flow to my brain. The lack of oxygen flow to the brain causes a loss of consciousness. My doctor believed implanting a pacemaker would resolve the issue. She was wrong.

The surgery was uneventful, and a few days later they released me from the hospital. I was healing well by the time Christmas morning arrived, happy to be home with my family. We enjoyed the usual opening of gifts, and I sat down to rest. I felt a harsh, stabbing pain in my chest, painful enough to cause me to scream. This got my attention. I laid down on the bed, assuming I had overexerted myself. About an hour later, I had another stabbing pain. As the day went on, the pain became more frequent and severe. By late afternoon, the pain was unbearable and happening every ten minutes, so I returned to the hospital. Again.

There aren't many doctors in the emergency room on Christmas Day, so it took a while to get a cardiac specialist to the ER. When the doctor arrived, he ran a few tests and found the issue. The leads of my pacemaker had dislodged from my heart. I was bleeding into my pericardium, the membrane that encloses the heart. I needed another surgery to repair the damage and reimplant the pacemaker leads into my heart. So back I went to the operating room. Again.

The recovery from the second pacemaker surgery was much harder. The cumulative effect of multiple surgeries was taking a toll. But within a few weeks I went back to work, and life was returning to normal.

One sunny morning in April, I woke up with a severe pain in my abdomen. With all my recent medical issues, I went to see my doctor to find out what was happening. She sent me to the hospital for some tests. Within the hour I was being prepped for surgery, this time to remove my gallbladder.

It had been six months of medical crisis. Losing consciousness in the kitchen, months of medical tests, cardiac arrest (twice), two pacemaker surgeries, and another surgery to remove my gallbladder. Now I was in a coma with twenty-four hours left to live.

I'm still alive, almost twelve years later, because something unexpected yet wonderful happened. The doctor suggested that my family consider placing me on the organ transplant list for a new liver. The odds weren't favorable. People often languish for years on the waiting list, but for reasons I can't explain, I made it to the top of the list right away. A few hours later, someone in Arizona died. Because they were an organ donor, and I was a suitable match, I received the gift of life.

Doctors in Arizona performed the delicate surgery to remove the donor's organs. They packed the liver I needed in ice, placed it on a jet, and flew it to Stanford Hospital in California. A team of talented surgeons performed a twelve-hour operation to transplant the donated liver into my body. It was the gift of a lifetime, the chance to watch my kids grow up.

The experience of almost dying left me with two clear takeaways—life is fragile, and life is precious. You can lose it all in a moment. I found a new appreciation for how special life is and felt a deeper urgency to make the most of my life. I didn't want any of it wasted. When the doctor told me I might die, all I could think about were the things I still wanted to do in my life. Now I had a second chance and the opportunity to appreciate it more than I had before.

In her poem "The Summer Day,"[1] Mary Oliver poses the question we should all ask ourselves regularly. "Tell me, what is it you plan to do with your one wild and precious life?" It's a question for which we should all have an answer and one we will explore throughout the rest of this book.

Why I'm Writing This Book

Looking back, I feel fortunate to have experienced all the health issues I did. While the pain, uncertainty, and fear were horrible, I feel lucky for the perspective I gained, and luckier still to be alive. How do you calculate the value of a second chance at life?

I think about dying every day, not in a morbid or fearful way, just cognizant that every morning I wake up is a bonus. I've been living in overtime for the last eleven years, nine months, and twenty-three days. Every year my family and I celebrate the anniversary of my transplant more than we celebrate my birthday. We reminisce about the experiences we've shared and the memories we've created over the past eleven years, aware that none of them would have happened without someone dying and giving me the chance to live. Life is fragile and precious. I never want to lose sight of that. Almost losing my life has given me clarity. I want to do everything I can to live my life to the fullest.

I'm writing this book for several reasons. First, not everyone will go through a life-or-death crisis. That puts them at risk for missing out on the perspective that comes with almost dying. I hope that by sharing my experience and perspective, others can benefit. I hope what I've learned can help you as you look to make the most of your one wild and precious life.

Another reason I'm writing this book is because perspective fades. I want to remind myself of the blessings and perspective I've received. I want to guard against complacency. Being mindful of the journey helps me keep what I've learned at the forefront of my mind and never forget the incalculable value of life.

And last, knowing the very fleeting nature of life, I wanted to document the journey so my kids, Aidan, Brendan, and Kylie, know the details of my story and can apply the lessons learned to their own lives. Some people wait their entire life before they examine the life they are living. I want my kids to pursue the life they want to live as early as possible. I hope they find ideas and encouragement in the pages that follow.

A Life Worth Living explores how to live an extraordinary life, one you'd be excited to live, a life with no regrets. We will dream big and imagine the possibilities of what your life could be. We'll unpack strategies for finding your purpose and establishing the practices that will help you live the life you want to live.

I hope you find inspiration that sparks a desire to make the most of your one wild and precious life. I hope you will take action with the ideas and strategies so you can live the life you want to live. Take the parts that resonate and leave the rest behind. One idea is enough to change your life. I hope you find several useful ideas here that help you make your life everything you imagined it could be.

PART I

THE LIFE YOU HAVE

Realize deeply that the present moment is all that you ever have.

—Eckhart Tolle

1

EVERYONE, EVERYWHERE

H*ome Alone* is one of my favorite holiday movies. It's about a precocious eight-year-old accidentally left home alone in Chicago when his family heads to Europe for a Christmas holiday. Once the parents realize they've left their youngest child, Kevin, home by himself, hilarity ensues as the family tries to get home to him.

There is a scene where the family is at Uncle Rob's house in France. The parents are making frantic phone calls, and the kids are discussing Kevin being home all by himself. Megan, Kevin's sister, expresses her concern:

Megan: You're not at all worried something might happen to him?

Buzz (*the oldest brother*): No. For three reasons: (a) I'm not that lucky, (2) we have smoke detectors, and (d) we live in the most boring street in the United States of

America, where nothing even remotely dangerous will ever happen. Period.[1]

That's kind of how I felt about my neighborhood growing up; calm and peaceful Campbell, California, population of 25,000. It was a typical middle-class neighborhood in the suburbs. Most of the neighbors were young families, so I had plenty of kids my age to play with. Four-bedroom houses lined the streets, all with a car or two in the driveway. People had decent jobs. Schools were good, the streets safe, and no one wanted for much.

Latimer Elementary School was around the corner from my house, and the neighborhood cabana club was a few blocks away. I spent most summer days splashing around in the pool with friends, and the rest of the time riding my bike, or playing baseball in the street. We caught Olympic fever during the 1976 Summer Olympic Games, holding our own neighborhood Olympics to coincide.

The best event was the high jump. Everyone dragged their mattresses from their bedrooms out to my front yard, stacking them three high to create a soft landing pit for the event. The drama reached epic proportions when we moved to the boxing competition. We created a boxing ring with garden hoses serving as the ropes and people standing as the corner posts to keep the hoses resembling the shape of a boxing ring. We drew pairs, donned boxing gloves, and did our best impressions of Sugar Ray Leonard, while trying to avoid getting knocked out in front of everyone in the neighborhood.

We had a lot of fun and laughter in my neighborhood. It

was a fantastic place to grow up. But even in the most idyllic places, pain and tragedy find their way in.

Michael lived a few houses down, just over my backyard fence. We were both in Mrs. Thompson's fifth grade class, and Michael's brother, Robert, was one grade older than us. The two brothers were amiable and well liked. They grew up in Hawaii and had that laid-back island vibe. They were brothers and also best friends.

One night near the end of our fifth grade year, wailing sirens interrupted the quiet evening. Michael and Robert had some friends over at their house. With their parents out to dinner, Robert wanted to show his friends his dad's gun. They gathered in a circle, Michael standing opposite Robert. Robert pointed the gun at the floor and pulled the trigger. He assumed the gun was empty, but there was a bullet in the chamber. Robert wasn't ready for the powerful kick that came when he pulled the trigger. The gun lurched backwards, and a moment later Michael collapsed to the floor. They were all surprised by the blast, so it took a moment for them to realize what happened. But it all became clear when they looked down and saw Michael lying in a pool of blood.

Michael died that night, and a part of Robert died with him. Killing his brother devastated Robert and left him crushed with guilt. I remember Mrs. Thompson trying to help me and my classmates make sense of it all, and I recall most of the class crying. Michael's house was across the street from our school. It was hard not to stare at his house, knowing the terrible things that had happened there the night before.

Kids in elementary school don't know how to cope with a tragedy like the death of a classmate. Many lashed out at Robert, blaming him for Michael's death, without realizing that Michael's death affected Robert more than it did anyone else. Robert never returned to school that year, and he was never quite the same after that.

I kept thinking, *Things like that don't happen in my neighborhood.* But they do. They happen everywhere. There is no place immune from tragedy and pain. Over the next dozen years, tragedy would frequently revisit my safe, happy, typical, middle-class neighborhood.

Another classmate, Rob, lived down the street, across from the cabana club. He got drunk one night and then drove home. He crashed into another car, killing the driver. Rob went to prison for manslaughter. A few years later, and just a few doors down from Rob's house, Chris and his girlfriend got into an argument. She pulled a gun and shot him. Another classmate gone.

My sophomore year in high school, I had a crush on Lisa. We had several classes together, and she was always so sweet and kind. She lived in the corner house across the street from the high school. After the school play one night, Lisa ran across the street to her house. She got hit by a car and died just a few feet from her front yard. The next day was another somber, grief-stricken day at the school. Another classmate gone, and more to come.

Tim and Gabe were in my class and they were best friends. On Thanksgiving night of our junior year, they thought it would be fun to go to the high school, drink some beers, and drive around the track. Gabe climbed on top of the car, and Tim started driving. Tim lost control of the car and crashed into the grandstand. Gabe flew off the roof of the car and into the cement wall of the grandstand. He died, and Tim spent the next five years in prison for killing his best friend.

Another somber day of grieving at the high school, and two more classmates gone.

Mark died in a motorcycle accident. Matt dropped dead walking out of the stadium after a Stanford football game. Frank, a star baseball player, got tangled up with drugs and ended up getting shot in a drug deal gone bad. Two of my closest friends attempted to kill themselves, one by pills, the other by hanging himself. They both survived, but Shane didn't. Shane and I were both on the wrestling team. We graduated high school together, and he joined the military. He killed himself a few months after boot camp when he found out he was being deployed to the Middle East. And Andy had the horrible experience of finding his father dead in the garage, locked in the car, engine still running.

It couldn't get much closer to home than the murder of my next-door neighbor Jeanine. Jeanine met a guy named Maurice at the Rock Bottom Restaurant & Brewery in downtown Campbell. She left the restaurant with him and was never seen again. The police found a blood-stained rug in a dumpster near Maurice's house, and they arrested him. But there was a mix-up at the lab, and the police had to release him because of a lack of usable evidence. The case dragged on for years. Police arrested Maurice a second time but released him again.

One night, over a decade since her disappearance, Jeanine's brother Wayne saw Maurice eating dinner at a restaurant. Wayne drove home, which was just a mile away. He grabbed a gun, drove back, and confronted Jeanine's suspected killer as he was leaving the restaurant. The two argued, Wayne shot and killed Maurice, and then as police arrived, Wayne killed himself.

Things like that don't happen in my neighborhood. But they do. Tragedy knows no boundaries, and no one is exempt from the pain. One need only look at the statistics to see that people are struggling. Life is hard. So many people are a million miles away from living the lives they wanted to or imagined.

The World Health Organization reports that 264 million people around the world suffer from depression, an increase of 60 percent over the past forty-five years. For some, life becomes so hopeless they choose suicide as their solution. Over 800,000 die by suicide every year, touching people from every walk of life. Suicide is now the second leading cause of death in fifteen-to-twenty-nine-year-olds.[2] Sheldon Kopp, a psychotherapist and author, summed it up well: "Life can be counted on to provide all the pain that any of us might need."

When life is difficult, it's easy to imagine we're all alone, suffering in ways nobody else can imagine. It's tempting to buy into the illusion that some people have it all. The rich and famous, the good looking, those lucky enough to have lives so much easier than ours. How untrue that can be. Everyone is hurting, and everyone has pain. Some just hide it better than others. One person more than any other helped me realize this. His name was Ricky Berry.

2

THE HAPPIEST GUY I EVER MET

Ricky and I both attended San Jose State University and had many of the same classes together. I noticed him right away because he was six feet eight and was always in a fantastic mood. While I was anxious about my quickly approaching and unavoidable entry into adulthood, Ricky seemed immune to it all. He was a carefree guy, and everything about his life seemed wonderful.

I always believed that life is difficult for everyone. But after watching Ricky live a charmed life during the two years I knew him, I wondered, *Maybe some people get to have it all.*

Ricky was a handsome, affable guy, always smiling and relaxed. He was a fantastic athlete, the career-leading scorer on our college basketball team. He had a beautiful girlfriend, a nice car, and lots of friends. While I was wrestling with the prospect of an uncertain future, Ricky's was clear. He was talented enough to play professional basketball. He would get drafted in the NBA, make a fantastic living doing something he loved, and live happily ever after.

Our final classes wrapped up, and we graduated. I was no closer to understanding what I would do with my life. The Sacramento Kings drafted Ricky in the first round. He had a solid rookie season, averaging 11 points per game, scoring a season high of 34 points against the Warriors, and was an outstanding three-point shooter. His future was bright. He married his beautiful girlfriend, bought a nicer car, and moved into a bigger house. He continued living his charmed and wonderful life.

I was living in a rundown neighborhood with four roommates and a dog in an 880-square-foot, two-bedroom house. I worked as a house painter to make ends meet. Not the future any of us aspired to.

It was August 14, my twenty-fourth birthday. I was on my way home, driving past the university where I rode the elevators and sat in class with Ricky, the happiest guy I'd ever met. That's when I heard the news on the radio. "Ricky Berry, NBA standout rookie for the Sacramento Kings, died of a self-inflicted gunshot to the head in his home in Sacramento."

It stunned me. How was that possible? Ricky had everything, the perfect life. I wasn't the only one shocked by the news. Martin McNeil of the *LA Times* wrote, "Berry's zest for life, combined with an apparently unlimited future, seemed to make him the least likely person to end his own life." Kevin Johnson, former NBA star and mayor of Sacramento, said, "If you look at his life, he had everything that you'd think would make somebody happy. He made a lot of money, had a beautiful wife, had a nice car, a nice home, a very promising career ahead of him, he was drug- and alcohol-free and in the prime of his life at 24 years old. What could he want?"[1]

Ricky's death had a big impact on me. How could I have been so wrong about his perfect life? Sometimes it's impossible to tell who is doing well and who isn't. I watched him for years and never saw a moment of struggle. And yet, life became so much for him that he felt it was better to end it than go on. I realized that some people may have opportunities that others do not, like more money or fame, but everyone, without exception, has pain and struggle in their life. Life is hard for everyone. Some just hide it better than others.

We get so fooled by the outward appearances, but we needn't look very far to realize that Ricky's situation is not unusual. History is littered with stories of people who "had it all" but still found life too hopeless to go on, people who appeared to have it all, right until the moment they ended their own lives.

When actor and comedian Robin Williams killed himself, it shocked the world. He looked so full of life, and he brought so much laughter to other people. Who could know how desperate he felt about his own life? Marilyn Monroe was the most famous woman in the world, but she felt alone and depressed. The list goes on, people from all walks of life: Anthony Bourdain (chef and TV personality), Kate Spade (fashion designer), Mark Rothko (abstract expressionist artist), Ernest Hemingway (American writer), Kurt Cobain (lead singer and guitarist for Nirvana). They all were so unhappy they opted out of life instead of living it. Everyone has pain in their life, even the rich and famous. Some are just better at hiding it.

But pain and difficulty are only part of the story. For as much suffering as there is in the world, there's an equal amount of joy, happiness, and beauty. Anatole France saw the full picture: "Life is delicious, horrible, charming, sweet, bitter, and that is everything." Everyone gets the gamut. No one can avoid pain, but you can live your life in such a way that you move through it, allow it to shape you, without being overwhelmed.

Anyone can create a life to see more of the wonder and beauty and experience less of the sadness and suffering. You can design a life that would thrill you to live. It's not about living a perfect, pain-free life or living a life better than anyone else. It's about living a life tomorrow that's better than the one you are living today. It's about making sure you find the delicious and charming sweet parts of life and enjoy them to the fullest. There is hope and adventure. A life worth living is waiting for you, and it begins with what you see.

3

THE GIFT OF PERSPECTIVE

After my transplant, when I was far enough past the crisis and I knew I would live, I reflected on my life. I saw it in an entirely new way. I was more grateful for simple things, things I wouldn't have spent two seconds thinking about in the past. I thought I was living through the worst year of my life, filled with surgeries and pain and uncertainty. But over time, I saw the whole experience as a gift. It was a difficult year and I wouldn't want to repeat any of it. But the perspective I gained was life changing. It gave me the gift of appreciation for life, how fragile and precious it is.

I realized there were many wonderful things around me, things I had stopped noticing and appreciating. It's easy to notice the difficulties and disappointments, but it doesn't mean the beautiful things aren't still there. I just had to pay attention and look for them. My health issues gave me a better perspective on how good my life was, and I was certain I would never lose sight of that again. I wouldn't let the little annoyances of life frustrate me or distract me from appreciating all that I had. I was wrong.

As my life returned to normal, I realized that annoying people are still annoying, terrible drivers are still frustrating, and inconsiderate people still made me angry. I realized I couldn't live off yesterday's perspective but needed to choose how I would see the world every day. If I were to live the life I wanted, I needed to be deliberate about choosing the actions that would yield the life I wanted to live. And I needed to make those choices again, every single day.

It's so easy to get stuck in the grind of everyday life. Kids, career, paying bills, washing dishes, buying groceries, holidays, then back to work. Rinse and repeat. Cars break down, people get sick. Sometimes I'm in a bad mood. I don't know why. Such is life. The challenges are endless and unceasing. It can be exhausting. How is anyone supposed to find the time to overcome so many challenges, or the energy to create an extraordinary life? The short answer is, one choice and one action at a time. It all begins with resetting your perspective.

The Ultimate Perspective

It's a large auditorium. There are 150 or 200 people gathered, some sitting, some standing. A slideshow of photographs projects onto a screen at the front of the hall. Soft music is playing, drowned out by the din of conversation. Many people you know, but not all. Stragglers sneak in the back door as a familiar face goes to the podium and welcomes everyone gathered.

There is singing and sharing, laughter and tears. People make their way to the microphone and tell stories of favorite memories. The stories have one thing in common. They're all about you. This is a celebration of life, a funeral. Yours. There are people gathered to say goodbye, sharing stories about the life you lived. When your life is over, what stories do you want told about you? What do you want people to remember?

Stories will be told about the life you lived, not the life you wanted to live. Are you living a life that will generate the stories you desire? Reflecting on the end of your life can help bring clarity to what's important. It can help you realize the gap between the life you are living and the life you want. In his blog post, *Seven Strange Questions That Help You Find Your Life Purpose,* Mark Manson wrote, "Ultimately, death is the only thing that gives us perspective on the value of our life."[1]

In South Korea, living funerals are a growing practice.[2] Participants write their last will and testament, then attend their own funeral ceremony. They wear funeral shrouds and lie in a closed coffin for ten minutes. The intent is to help people contemplate their death so they will come away with a fresh perspective on their life.

One participant, Cho, was seventy-five years old when she held a living funeral for herself. She said, "Once you become conscious of death and experience it, you undertake a new approach to life." By putting themselves at the end of life's journey, participants can identify relationships that need mending, words that need speaking. With this fresh perspective, they have the chance to change their lives before it's too late.

It's a worthwhile exercise to spend an hour reflecting on the end of your life. How do you feel about the life you've lived so far? What are your hopes and dreams for the days you have left? Being Irish, I feel I have an advantage because the Irish are seasoned funeral-goers. I've attended scores of funerals, of people I knew very well and many I'd never met. Irish people go to funerals of anyone who even resembles a friend or acquaintance. The conversations with my mom about someone's funeral usually went something like this:

Mom: You know Mary?
Me: Who?
Mom: Mary O'Malley.
Me: No.
Mom: You do.
Me: Who is she?
Mom: She's married to Michael.
Me: Which one is Michael?
Mom: They're from Dublin.
Me: I don't remember them.
Mom: You do. They were part of the Irish Club.
Me: Okay. What about her?
Mom: Her nephew died.
Me: Did I know him?
Mom: I don't think so.
Me: Okay.
Mom: The funeral is tomorrow morning at 10:00 a.m.

Translation: Mary is from Ireland. My mother knows her, but I don't, at least I don't recall ever meeting her. If we met, it was most likely at someone's funeral. Her nephew, who I'm certain I've never met, died. We are Irish. Irish people go to funerals. I should be at my mom's house by nine o'clock in the morning to go with her to Mary's nephew's funeral.

This scene happened dozens of times during my life. And as strange as it is to attend the funeral of someone you don't know, I always found it a meaningful experience. It makes you think about life. You hear about the moments others found memorable and noteworthy. You get a glimpse into what people valued, and you see the profound ways one person can affect others over a lifetime. The stories take you on a journey to the important and memorable moments of life. Moments of joy and laughter, sorrow and celebration. But there is always one underlying sentiment. Life is temporary. It will end. Funerals remind us to reflect. They encourage us to ask the ever-important question—*What are you doing with your one wild and precious life?*

Whatever way you do it, spend some time thinking about the end of your life. Maybe it will give you clarity on how you want to live. But unlike your actual funeral, you get to go back to your life and decide what you will do with the days you have left to live. There is tremendous power in perspective when you begin with the end in mind. The end of your life can motivate you to make more of the moments you have left.

4

HOW WILL YOU BE REMEMBERED?

Alfred Nobel had a profound experience reflecting on his life and the legacy he would leave when he died. He grabbed his morning newspaper, sat at his dining room table, and read the news of his own death. There, on the front page, was the shocking headline announcing to the world that he was dead.

It was, in fact, Alfred's brother Ludwig who died, but a French newspaper believed it was Alfred. As a result, the newspaper ran their obituary of Alfred Nobel rather than Ludwig Nobel. And what Alfred read about himself horrified him.

Nobel was a chemist, businessman, engineer, and inventor. He had over 350 patents to his name and achieved many notable accomplishments in his life. We associate Nobel with the Nobel Prizes, the Nobel Peace Prize in particular.

People in his day would have found that laughable.

Of his 355 patents, Nobel was most famous for his work with nitroglycerin and his invention of dynamite. This patent alone made him a wealthy man. Despite his many accomplishments, it shook Alfred to see how the newspaper headline summarized his life:

The Merchant of Death is Dead

"Dr. Alfred Nobel, who became rich by finding ways
to kill more people faster than ever before, died
yesterday."[1]

It horrified Nobel to see his life's work attributed to death and destruction. This was not the legacy he imagined for himself. He wanted much more. Now that he had seen the reality of his reputation, Nobel would change his story.

Alfred committed himself to improving the world and society. He drafted his will, leaving 94 percent of his fortune to set up the Nobel Prizes that would recognize the greatest achievements of mankind. He chose five areas of study he believed could most benefit humanity: Physics, Chemistry, Physiology or Medicine, Literature, and Peace. The Nobel Committee later added a sixth prize for Economic Sciences. Since its inception, the Nobel Foundation has awarded prizes to over nine hundred people.[2]

Alfred Nobel's desire to change his legacy drove him to take action that continues to enable new generations to make a lasting impact on mankind. He is no longer remembered as the Merchant of Death. The world remembers him now as the creator of the Nobel Peace Prize.

If Alfred Nobel could change his legacy, so can you. Even if your life is a total disaster, you can write a better story and create the ending you want. It's not what you've done that matters, but what you do from this point forward. Every day is a new beginning. Every day is a chance to start again. You can change the outcome of your life in a moment by choosing to move in a new direction.

What headline do you want for your life? Your story is not done being written. It's not too late to change the ending. How do you want to be remembered?

5

REGRET

Alfred Nobel had a moment of clarity. He realized his life was not what he wanted it to be, and he changed his story. Almost twelve years ago, when I was close to dying, I realized I hadn't done all I wanted to do with my life. I was fortunate to get a second chance, the opportunity to live a better life, one without the regret of dying with so much still to do.

Steven Pressfield said, "Most of us have two lives. The life we live, and the unlived life within us."[1] I realized how much unlived life I still had in me, and I'm grateful I now get to live it. When my life is over, I don't want any unlived life left in me. I want to live it all, soak it up, and experience life to the fullest. I want to know that I faced my fears, pushed through my insecurities, overcame my doubts, and had the courage to pursue my dreams. I want to know I gave it everything I had.

When I look around, I see many people who aren't passionate about the lives they are living. They take for granted their days, assuming there will be an endless supply of tomorrows. There isn't. Our stories will all end, and many won't like the story they leave behind.

Bronnie Ware was a palliative care nurse in Australia. Her job was to work with patients living with a serious illness. This often involved patients who were dying. Bronnie was with patients during the last days of their lives. She saw first-hand how people faced their own mortality, how they struggled with their unresolved issues. She saw how patients came to terms with death, but she also noticed that many shared one particular commonality: regret. Not only did they have regrets, but they had the same regrets. She writes about her findings in her book *The Top Five Regrets of the Dying*. This is what she heard.

The Top Five Regrets of the Dying:

1. I wish I'd had the courage to live a life true to myself, not the life others expected of me.
2. I wish I hadn't worked so hard.
3. I wish I'd had the courage to express my feelings.
4. I wish I had stayed in touch with my friends.
5. I wish I had let myself be happier.[2]

If you died tomorrow, which of these regrets would you have? Would you still have some unlived life inside you, dreams left unpursued? Teddy Roosevelt said, "Far better it is to dare mighty things, to win glorious triumphs, even though checkered by failure, than to take rank with those poor spirits who neither enjoy much nor suffer much, because they live in the gray twilight that knows not victory nor defeat."[3] Dare to do mighty things with your life. Choosing to live in the gray twilight will never yield the life you've always imagined. It will yield regret.

There's still time to write a better story, time to live the life you want to live. You are the writer and director of your life. If it isn't what you want it to be, then change it. You get to choose the adventures you will pursue. You get to choose the character you will become. It's time to move from the life you have to the life you want.

PART II

THE LIFE YOU WANT

Wish not so much to live long as to live well.

—Benjamin Franklin

6

WHAT'S YOUR STORY?

What story are you living right now? Is it memorable? Inspiring? Disappointing? Is it the life you imagined living? All of us have a unique journey of our own, shaped by circumstance, events and people. Are you satisfied with the life you are living?

We get to decide whether we live a life that's remarkable or ordinary. We choose the story our lives will tell. Maya Angelou said, "There is no greater agony than bearing an untold story inside you." Are you telling your story? Or is it still inside you, waiting to be lived? We get to decide whether we live a remarkable life, but many people opt for the ordinary, or at least settle for it.

To know where you want to go, it's important to look back on where you've been. The events of our childhood shaped us. We developed patterns and behaviors to navigate our lives as best as we could. We picked up habits and strategies for survival, some positive and others destructive. We look to the past not for excuses but for clues on how to live our best life going forward. Events in my childhood shaped me and still influence how I want to live my life now.

The Beginning

I assumed my experience growing up was normal because it was normal to me. Sure, I noticed some kids had parents less strict than mine, or got to eat out more often, but we all seemed to go about life the same way. It wasn't until much later that I realized there's no such thing as normal. Everybody has things in common, but every person lives their own unique life, shaped by their own distinct experiences. I appreciate how ordinary and extraordinary my life has been.

My mom and dad were born, raised, and married in Ireland. They made the life-changing decision to move to America. Life changing for them and for me. I wouldn't be the same person I am today if they had stayed in Ireland. I'm grateful they came to America.

They arrived in San Francisco as newlyweds. They lived with my dad's sister and her husband in a small apartment. Soon my sister, Linda, was born, then three years and one day later I joined the family. I remember little from my time in San Francisco—a few friends, and some vague memories of the stairs leading up to the house. I wasn't there long.

When I was four years old, my mom, sister, and I went back to Ireland for a vacation. My dad stayed in San Francisco. Weeks turned into months, and I remember asking when we were going home. My mom told me there was an airplane strike and there weren't any planes to bring us home. We ended up staying in Ireland for almost a year.

I later realized that a yearlong airplane strike never happened and learned the real story. When my mom and dad arrived in the United States, they had next to nothing. My dad worked several jobs, sweeping coffee off the floor at the Folgers coffee plant, doing janitorial work, and tending bar. He started drinking too much and at some point, my mom had had enough. She took me and my sister back to Ireland to live with her father. To my dad's credit, he got sober and stopped drinking. My mom gave their marriage another try. We moved back to Campbell, California, to the safe and boring neighborhood where I thought nothing bad would ever happen.

The Early Years

Returning from Ireland had its challenges. In the previous twelve months I'd lived in San Francisco, Kilkenny, and now Campbell. I joined my kindergarten class halfway through the school year, so I was the new kid who didn't know anyone.

Because I was quiet and shy, it was hard for me to make friends. Trusting new people wasn't easy. Fear was a big part of my childhood. I was small and skinny, which made me a tempting target for bullies at school and in my neighborhood.

Mitch lived five houses down. He was three years older than me, and he was a big kid. He gave me a hard time and liked to push me around if I ever went near his house. I don't know what I did to earn his wrath, but I was careful to avoid his part of the street.

Despite my size, I was a good athlete. I played several sports, including Little League baseball. Like every other kid I started in Tee Ball my first year. Before my second year I went through the usual baseball tryouts. It surprised me when a minor league team selected me. Almost all second-year players played in the C league, where they experienced fast-pitch baseball for the first time. So rather than making the change to fast-pitch baseball with other beginners, I was playing with seasoned players in the minor league.

I remember very little except being afraid. I hated stepping into the batter's box to face a pitcher throwing a baseball as hard as he could in my direction. I feared being hit by the ball whether I was batting or playing left field. Somehow I played well, but I was anxious the entire time I was on the field.

One year later, a major league team drafted me. I was the youngest and smallest kid by far. The pitching was even faster, and the other players even bigger and stronger than before. I felt like I was in the land of giants.

Two of those giants were Mark and Mario, and they found great delight in picking on me. They were mean and relentless. I can still see their snarling faces that intimidated me so much. I was too afraid to tell anyone, so I quit instead. The coaches were kind and had a good idea what was happening. They told me how much potential they saw in me, which is why they had picked me for the team even though I was so young. They wanted me to stay on the team and challenged me to stick it out. So I did.

The team was going on a camping trip, and while I had stayed on the team, there was no way I was heading into the woods with the bullying Neanderthals. So I stayed home. And in one of those simple but meaningful moments of life,

Mr. Roberts, the dad of our star player, took me to my first Major League Baseball game to see the San Francisco Giants. It was a kind gesture to help me feel I wasn't missing out, and one I still appreciate forty years later.

I stayed on the team, endured the taunting and bullying from Mark and Mario, but also gained confidence and skill. In my third and last season with the team, the coaches selected me as the Most Valuable Player. It taught me a good lesson in staying the course even when things get difficult.

I had grown more confident, but I was still a kid afraid to step up to bigger challenges. The following year I was too old for Little League, so I would have to play in a more competitive league for older kids. Despite ending Little League with an MVP season, I opted out of playing baseball in the Pony League and ended my baseball years. Fear was still holding me back.

These events from my childhood shaped me. When I looked at my story, I didn't like a lot of what I saw. I realized that I needed to overcome my fears and learn to trust people more if I was to live a better life. I needed to step up and face bigger challenges, even if they made me uncomfortable. I needed to learn to take action and not be so passive about my life.

Your Life Right Now

Reflecting on your story will help you understand the parts of your life you like and those you'd like to change. From there you can determine the goals that will help you create the life you want to live.

We decide who we want to be and what we want to do with our lives. We get to choose who we are and how we behave. Everyone gets to design the life they want to live. That requires you to understand where you've been and the shaping events of your life. Then you will be better able to decide what is necessary to become the person you want to be. Then you will be ready to design the life you want to live.

What's your story? Give yourself time to consider the following questions, to ground yourself on where you are so you will have a better sense of where you'd like to be. Take out a pen and notebook and capture your thoughts.

- What about your life do you like?
- Which moments have you enjoyed the most?
- What do you dislike about your life?
- If you could change one thing, what would it be?
- Who do you enjoy spending time with?
- What do you find enjoyable about the time you spend with them?
- Who do you least enjoy spending time with?
- If it's unenjoyable, why are you spending time with them?
- Who do you admire, and what about them do you find admirable?
- On a scale of 1–10, how exciting is the story you are living right now?
- If you died tomorrow, would the life you lived satisfy you?

Understanding the answers to these questions serves as a starting point for designing a life you'd be excited to live. It can provide insights into beliefs and behaviors you need to overcome so you can make your life what you want it to be. You can see the impact people have in your life, how they can make things better or worse, the activities that bring you joy and excitement. This is a great foundation for dreaming big about what you want from your life.

7

DREAM BIG

W hat are you capable of achieving? Nelson Mandela said, "There is no passion to be found playing small —in settling for a life that is less than the one you are capable of living." Are you playing small with your life? Are you settling? If your life was everything you wished it could be, what would it look like?

As we get older, we sometimes forget to keep dreaming big, or keep dreaming at all. We lower our expectations and accept mediocrity. We play it safe to avoid disappointment and accept that this is life. It's a life, but it's not the best that your life can be. If you want to live an extraordinary life, one you'd be excited to live, dream big.

If you found a magic lamp, and the genie offered you the life of your dreams, would you be able to describe it? Not some vague generalities, but the specifics of what you'd consider your perfect life? If you don't know where you're going, how can you ever arrive? Roman Stoic philosopher Seneca said, "Our plans miscarry because they have no aim.

When a man does not know what harbor he is making for, no wind is the right wind." To live a remarkable life, you need to know what you're aiming for.

Don't buy into someone else's dream. This is personal. What's perfect for me won't be the same for you, nor should it be. This is your one wild and precious life. Don't play small. It's time to dream big and imagine what's possible with your life.

Designing Your Life

How remarkable can your life be? Tony Robbins said, "Make your life a masterpiece: Step beyond the demands of the moment and begin right now to design and live the life you deserve." Are you designing your life or living in the demands of the moment?

To live an extraordinary life you have to design it. You have to define what extraordinary looks like for you. Imagine the possibilities. Let go of the constraints and doubts that hold you back. Let yourself dream about the best your life can be.

The goal is to get your thoughts written. It doesn't have to be perfect. It's a starting point to help you consider a life you'd be excited to live. You may find yourself tempted to only list the goals you feel are attainable. Resist that temptation. Don't filter and don't hold back. Dream big and imagine your life if it was everything you wanted it to be.

Think of this as an investment in your future. Writing will help you clarify the details. It will help you reflect on what's most important to you. If you don't have a clear picture of your perfect life, you won't live it. Vague ideas about a wonderful life won't translate to anything remarkable. Without clarifying the details, you will always wonder if you are living your best life or settling for something less than was possible. Clarity is the start of designing the life you want. If you don't have fifteen minutes to invest in your future, you don't have time to live a remarkable life.

We'll begin by exploring the things you would like to have, the stuff you feel would make your life extraordinary. We're starting with this because it's easy, and not because it's most important. Of the five regrets Bronnie Ware saw in her dying patients, owning a Lamborghini didn't make the list. Consider this a warm-up for the more important ideas to come.

What Would You Like to Have? Make a list of fifty things you would like to own. Whatever you think would be important for you to live your best life. Don't hold back. Maybe you've dreamed of the house with the white picket fence or a cottage by the beach. Maybe for you, it's books and baseball cards. Write it down. Perhaps a Harley-Davidson or a convertible sports car. Which one? Be specific. A Porsche 911? A restored '67 Mustang? Add it to the list. Get creative. Maybe a special bottle of wine or a bicycle built for two.

My list included a Rickenbacker electric guitar and a baby grand piano so I can make music every day. And I want to have milk in my refrigerator, always. My family didn't have a lot of money when I was growing up, and milk was expensive and always in short supply. Sometimes we resorted to powdered milk, which I hated. I was jealous of the kids who had to drink a glass of milk with their dinner because that wasn't something I was allowed to do. My perfect life has a well-stocked refrigerator with plenty of ice-cold, 2 percent milk so I can enjoy a tall glass of milk whenever I want.

Is there something from your childhood that would be meaningful for you to have? Maybe your parents didn't permit pets. Your perfect life may include the puppy you never convinced them to get you, that basset hound with the huge, long ears and the droopy eyes. What would add color to your life? A personal library, an autographed Willie Mays baseball card, or a vegetable garden in the backyard? Remember, this is your list, not a one-size-fits-all list applicable to anyone. It's personal to you. Keep writing until you list at least fifty things.

Where Would You Like to Go? Travel may be the easiest way for you to add adventure and excitement to your life. This well-known anonymous quote sums it up well: "We travel not to escape life, but for life not to escape us." If you want to create a remarkable life, consider how travel might add to your story.

What places would you like to visit? What sights would you like to see? Make a list of your desired destinations. Maybe you'd like to walk the world's most beautiful beaches or climb the tallest peaks. Consider visiting the cosmopolitan cities of the world like New York, San Francisco, Paris, and London. You can travel to see the world's most amazing structures such as the Pyramids, the Roman Colosseum or the Great Wall of China. If you're looking for something more personal, think about visiting the country of your ancestors.

I love history and stories of the past. The second world war shaped history, revealing the worst and the best in humanity. Last year I visited the beaches of Normandy, the destination at the top of my travel list. I wanted to walk the beaches of D-Day and see the place where so many died in the fight between good and evil. It was a powerful experience that gave me a deeper appreciation for the peaceful times in which I live.

What do you want to see? Add to your life by visiting the country of your ancestors or walking the paths of history. Brave the Bermuda Triangle, or sail the seven seas. There are amazing sights to see all around the world—the Taj Mahal in India, Australia's Great Barrier Reef, the Tower of London, or Machu Picchu in Peru. Every country has something worth seeing. Don't let life slip away without seeing what you can of the world.

Memorable stories and movies draw on the common theme of an adventurous quest. You can elevate the role of travel in your life by making it an adventurous quest. My wife Vicky, the kids, and I have a goal to see all fifty states in America. Every year we pick a few we've not yet seen and we hit the road. I've realized that fifty is a lot. But with each state we visit, we are one step closer to completing our quest. So far, we've been to thirty-two states, and we've found interesting adventures in every one. But the sum is greater than its parts. It's the quest to see all fifty that's made the pursuit so special.

Living a remarkable life requires action. If you want to live life to the fullest, then you've got to leave the comfort of your couch and go. Somewhere, anywhere. Leave your routine and see the wonders of the world. They are waiting for you.

Who Would You Like to Meet? The world is full of interesting people, and they all have a unique story. You can add color to your life by spending time with new and interesting people. Who would you be excited to meet? Maybe you'd like to meet the CEO of your company, or get the autograph of a favorite movie star. Would you enjoy speaking with a scientist you admire? Write it down. Your list could include athletes or authors, politicians or poets. Whoever they may be, there's excitement in getting to meet people you find interesting.

Who would you put on your list? You are weaving the tapestry of your life, and the people you meet along the way are an interesting part of the story. Dream a little. Who would you like to meet?

What Would You Like to Do? Life is a collection of experiences. Are you collecting well? To live a remarkable life, there must be adventure and noteworthy experiences. In your perfect life, what do you want to experience? Skydiving? Hover above the world in a hot-air balloon? You can ride motorcycles and horses, roller coasters and waves. You can raft in white-watered rivers or run with the bulls in Pamplona. Explore an amazing world underwater by scuba diving or snorkeling. What you do is less important than doing something.

Do you prefer the great indoors? Then learn to knit or play the guitar. Write a book or learn to bake. The key is to experience what you've not experienced before. Every few years I learn to play a new instrument to add to my collection of life experiences. What's still on my list? Playing the bagpipes. I'm getting to know my neighbors better before I assault them with warbling and wailing pipes. What do you want to try? Get creative. Read a thousand books, build a house, paint landscapes, write poems, research your family history. The list is endless, so don't let yourself run out of possibilities. What can you try that will add to your life's story?

What Do You Want to Give? We know what we want. At least we think we do. The entire advertising industry exists to convince you to buy things you don't need and make you aware of what's missing from your life. But possessions aren't what make life meaningful. They aren't even near the top of the list of important things. Life takes on an extra level of meaning when we think beyond ourselves and focus on those around us.

Winston Churchill, the prime minister of England during WWII, said, "We make a living by what we get. We make a life by what we give." Making a remarkable life is what this book is about. If you want to design a life that is extraordinary, one that is filled with purpose, it has to include giving. Who do you want to help? What causes do you want to support? You get to decide what is meaningful to you. How might you give to affect the world and people around you?

Giving money is a helpful way to get involved, but it goes much further. Where will you give your time? To whom will you give words of encouragement and support? You can give people your undivided attention. You can give someone life-long memories by doing memorable activities together, things they've never done, in ways they never imagined. The more creative, the better. You can give grace when someone falters, forgiveness to those who need it. Give up your seat or give someone a second chance. There are countless ways to give. Find what works for you.

Sometimes I hear people say they wish they could give more. They want to contribute, but money is tight. Don't get caught up in the gift's size. You can grow into giving bigger gifts later. It's the practice that matters. You get good at giving by giving. Start small, but start now.

Normal people who didn't make a lot of money made an enormous impact with the gifts they gave. Genevieve Via Cava taught special needs students in New Jersey's Dumont school district for almost forty-five years. When she died, she left $1 million to her special needs students. She wanted to continue to care for them.[1] Ronald Read spent his career as a gas station attendant. He wanted giving to be a part of his story. When he died, he shocked his community by leaving $6 million to the local library and hospital.[2] Alan Naiman was a social worker in Washington state. He lived an unassuming, frugal life, drove old cars, wore old shoes, and ate at inexpensive restaurants. Alan donated $11 million to organizations that cared for kids who were sick, abandoned, or disabled because he wanted to help those who couldn't help themselves.

What's interesting about Alan Naiman is how his plans changed. He was planning to buy a house with a beautiful view and take some relaxing vacations. Then doctors told Alan he had terminal cancer. Instead of spending his last days seeing the world, he spent his time researching worthy charities. He decided he wanted his story to be about helping others, and he wanted to make sure he gave his money to the charities that could make the greatest impact.[3]

You can add to your story by giving extraordinary gifts. You can have an impact with your time and money and the gifts you give. Put at least as much effort into dreaming big about your giving goals as you did thinking about the places you want to visit. You make a life by what you give.

Two Gifts I Will Always Remember

Of all the memorable gifts I've received in my life, two come to mind, a bike and a pair of shoes. It wasn't the value of the gifts but the sentiment behind them that made them so meaningful.

When I was about ten years old, BMX bikes were all the rage. I was the only kid in the neighborhood who didn't have one. If there's something that makes you feel you don't belong, it's being the one kid standing on the sidewalk watching everyone else racing up and down the street on their bikes and then disappearing around the corner, heading off to adventures without you.

Murray lived across the street. He was a gruff airplane mechanic. One day he called me over to his garage and said, "Here, this is for you," pointing down at a BMX bike. He saw me watching the other kids riding their bikes, so he gathered up spare parts and assembled one for me. I've gone to see Murray several times over the last few decades to thank him for that bike. He's an old man now. But every time I remind him of his gift, he gets a big, broad smile and says, "Yeah, you needed a bike." It was an incredible gift.

I received the second gift from a colleague early in my career. When I first started working in high tech, one of the software engineers, Louis, wasn't performing well. His manager and I tried to help him improve his performance, but his skills weren't sufficient to do the complex work we were doing. The manager decided he needed to fire Louis.

We met with Louis and told him we were ending his employment. It was hard news for him to hear. The manager left, and I stayed with Louis. We talked about next steps and I offered to help him in any way I could. We talked for quite a while. Louis did most of the talking and I listened. I stayed with him until he was ready to go home.

A few days later I received a note from Louis thanking me for treating him with kindness and with respect. He appreciated the time I spent with him and how I listened. Louis knew I was planning on running a marathon. As a token of his appreciation, he gave me a pair of running shoes. He wanted to support me on my journey as I had supported him on his. It was a thoughtful and personal gesture. Never did I expect to receive a gift for firing someone. It reminded me that there are countless ways to give meaningful gifts. The more personal, the better.

What are some of the most meaningful gifts you've received? An unexpected, thoughtful, personalized gift can stay with you throughout your life. You have the power to affect people with the gifts you give. What will you give and to whom? You can improve your life story by making giving a central part of your life.

A Gift to Consider

As you consider ways you'd like to give, I want to suggest a unique gift. It may be the most meaningful gift you ever give . . . the gift of life. You can give someone—in fact, many people—the gift of life by becoming an organ donor. This is near to me as I wouldn't be alive today if it weren't for the person in Arizona who donated their organs. Their gift saved my life.

In the US alone, there are approximately 40,000 life-saving organ transplants performed each year. But there are over

100,000 people still waiting for a transplant, with another person in need added to the list every ten minutes. Twenty people die every day, still waiting.[4] You could save the life of someone on that list and make it possible for a little girl to spend many more years with her daddy, a husband to have more moments with his wife, a parent to get the gift of watching their child grow up.

By becoming an organ donor, you create the possibility of helping someone live. You can give the gift of life after you die. It costs you nothing, but the upside is priceless. Not only can you save someone's life, but your gift affects the lives of everyone they know. You can give families more time together, allow fathers to walk their daughters down the aisle. You can give the gift of lifelong memories of shared experiences that would otherwise be impossible. There are many organizations you can register with to be a donor. As you think about the role that giving will play in your life, consider giving the gift of life by becoming an organ donor. You may find that your last gift is the most meaningful gift you ever gave.

8

WELCOME TO THE ARENA

When you take the time to imagine what an extraordinary life yours can be, the possibilities should excite you. But not everyone will be excited about or supportive of your efforts to create a remarkable life. In fact, some people will do all they can to dissuade you from pursuing the life you have imagined for yourself. Some will have good intent, believing they have your best interest in mind. Others can't help but criticize because tearing people down is the only way they feel good about themselves.

The well intended fear you will dream mighty dreams and have your hopes dashed if your plans don't come to fruition. They prefer to play it safe and not risk disappointment. To see someone imagine amazing possibilities becomes a list of potential failures and defeats. Despite their good intentions, their advice is missing a key consideration. At the end of your life, you and you alone will look back on your life and determine whether it was the life you wanted to live. If there are regrets, they will be yours alone.

It's important to realize there will also be people who try to discourage you, not from a place of concern, but from a place of malice. These are the people who only feel big by making others feel small. They don't want you to succeed or thrive because they want to appear stronger, better, and more successful than you. It's easier for them if you give up and settle for a mediocre, half-lived life. But this isn't about you. The people who tear others down aren't interested in you living an extraordinary life. They fear people who are living fulfilling and exciting lives because it forces them to see they are not. So they critique and criticize, mock and discourage.

Teddy Roosevelt's speech The Man in the Arena captures the mindset we should have when dealing with people trying to tear us down:

> It is not the critic who counts; not the man who points out how the strong man stumbles, or where the doer of deeds could have done them better. The credit belongs to the man who is actually in the arena, whose face is marred by dust and sweat and blood; who strives valiantly, who errs and comes short again and again because there is no effort without error and shortcoming, but who does actually strive to do the deeds; who knows great enthusiasms, the great devotions; who spends himself in a worthy cause, who at the best knows in the end the triumph of high achievement, and who at the worst, if he fails, at least fails while daring greatly, so that his place shall never be with those cold and timid souls who neither know victory nor defeat.[1]

When you have the courage to dream and take steps to create the life you want to live, you step into the arena. Expect to meet critics. Disregard them. You have one wild and precious life. Don't let the critics dissuade you from living it the way you want. No matter how successful you are, you will never please everyone. Living your life trying to please others is a sure path to misery. Live your own life. Make it what you want it to be. Make it remarkable, regardless of what others say.

While I was writing this book, I had to remind myself what it means to step into the arena. It's easy to imagine the voices of the critics, *Who are you to write a book about living an extraordinary life? What makes you think your life is so remarkable?* Then I remember that it's not the critic that counts. I'm reminded that I don't want to let fear keep me from doing what I want to do and living the life I want to live. I know I would rather fail trying than fail to try. And so I write, knowing I at least free myself from the regret of wondering, *What if I had written?*

Some people try to find the middle ground. They try to live a remarkable life and avoid the critics. They want to be in the arena but encounter no resistance. Aristotle knew this to be impossible: "There is only one way to avoid criticism: do nothing, say nothing, and be nothing." The cost of avoiding criticism is too high. Face the critics. Live your life. Do. Say. Be. Try. Only then will you be able to live the life you want to live.

9

DON'T SETTLE FOR LESS

Perhaps you aren't sure what you want out of life. It's a deep question. Pick something, anything, so you have a destination in mind. If you decide later there are better destinations, better pursuits waiting, you can always change course. In the meantime, determine a destination for your life and fight for it. Don't settle. We can learn a lot about fighting for what you want from Sylvester Stallone. As a young man, he knew what he wanted, and he refused to settle for less.

Before Stallone was a household name, he was a struggling actor, struggling husband, and all-around struggling man. He was an actor without many acting gigs, which meant he was more or less unemployed. He continued to look for acting jobs, and his bank account continued to dwindle. Struggling, Sly pawned some of his wife's jewelry. This didn't help his struggling marriage, and soon the divorce was underway.[1] With his bank account balance hovering just above a hundred dollars, struggling to pay bills or buy food, Stallone came to one of the toughest decisions in his life. He didn't have enough money to buy dog food for his dog. So Stallone walked to a nearby 7-Eleven to find someone who would take care of his dog. He ended up selling Butkus for $40, and Stallone went home alone after watching his dog walk off with a stranger.[2] This was a new low.

Since his house didn't have heat, Stallone was spending his days in the public library. He found a discarded book on the table, one by Edgar Allan Poe, and he read it. Sly found Poe's words powerful, and they inspired him to write his own stories. One night Stallone was at home watching a boxing match on TV, a bout between the heavyweight champion Mohammed Ali and his challenger, the scrappy, unknown Chuck Wepner. Ali won the fight, but Wepner amazed the crowd with his determination and never-give-up persistence. Wepner's performance inspired Stallone. He spent the next twenty hours writing a screenplay about a nobody, down-on-his-luck boxer who got a shot at the title. Stallone poured himself into the story and saw it as a chance to write a role for himself that was deeply personal and one to which he could relate.

With the screenplay finished, Stallone sent it out, and against the odds, he found studios were interested. He received an offer of $125,000 for the script. With almost nothing in the bank, it was an amazing amount of money. And he turned it down. Why? Because he had one condition that the filmmakers wouldn't agree to. Stallone insisted that he be the star of the movie. He was an actor at heart, and this screenplay was a chance for him to get a role he felt destined to play. The studio wasn't interested in taking a chance on a no-name actor. And they parted ways.

A few weeks later, the studio called Stallone with an offer

of $250,000 for his script. Again, they didn't want Stallone as the lead in the movie, so he turned down their offer again. The studio came back a third time, offering $350,000. But the issue remained. They didn't want Stallone in the movie. Sly knew what he wanted, and he wouldn't settle for less. He walked away from their offer. It shows an incredible amount of clarity and conviction to have $100 to your name and still walk away from $350,000. But Stallone knew what he wanted, and he didn't compromise. His conviction paid off.

The studio came back a fourth time, figuring something was better than nothing. They decided they would make the movie on a low budget. They offered Stallone a paltry $35,000 and a percentage of the box office for the script, but this time Stallone would play the lead role.[3] Instead of making a big-budget, Hollywood blockbuster with Ryan O'Neal or Burt Reynolds as the studios had intended, they made the movie with a no-name star for $1 million. No one expected much.

The movie, *Rocky*, was a smash hit. It made more than $200 million at the box office. It received nine Oscar nominations and won three, including the Oscar for Best Picture. And because Stallone had a percentage of the unexpectedly successful box office, he made millions. The character Rocky Balboa would become the foundation of Stallone's long and successful acting career.

None of this would have happened if Sylvester Stallone wasn't clear about what he wanted. He saw himself as an actor, and the most important thing, far more important than the money, was the chance to play the lead in the movie. I wonder what would have happened if he had taken the $350,000 and not played the part of Rocky Balboa. Would Stallone be the star he is today? Would the movie have been a success? Would there be a *Rocky II* and *III*, and *IV* and *V* and . . . ? It made a world of difference that Stallone knew exactly what he wanted, and he went after it. Do you know what you want?

Interestingly enough, there was something else Stallone knew he wanted. His dog. It broke his heart to sell Butkus. So when he received the check for $35,000 for the *Rocky* script, he went back to the 7-Eleven where he had last seen his dog. He waited until the man who bought Butkus showed up. Stallone approached the man and told him he wanted to buy his dog back. Sly recalls, "The new owner knew I was desperate and charged me $15,000. He was worth every penny!"[4] To some it would be insane to pay $15,000 for a dog, particularly one you sold for only $40 a few months earlier. It all depends on what's important to you. There is a cost to everything we want. But if it's something you really desire, it's worth the price.

If you know what you want out of life, fight for it. Don't settle for less. Go after it with everything you have because there is no next time. Not all pursuits are equal. Don't waste your time and energy on the less important stuff. Your time and resources are limited. But gaining clarity on what's important to you will help you put your energy into the right things. Johann Wolfgang von Goethe is said to have written, "Things that matter most must never be at the mercy of things that matter least." Decide what matters most to you, and then go after it with the same determination Stallone went after the part of Rocky Balboa, with the same resolve he had to get his dog back. The story of your life will be better for it.

10

GETTING STARTED

Y ou've considered your life. You've decided you'd rather suffer the pain of discipline than the pain of regret. You've thought about the life you want to live, how it would look if everything was exactly the way you'd like it to be. You know you've got to take action to create the life you want. You can begin with one step, but what step do you take? It doesn't matter. Action, followed by more action, will build momentum, and provided you know what you are trying to accomplish, you'll eventually find your way. Just take a step and then take another. The most important thing is getting started.

Start small and begin by taking practical steps. Sometimes we overthink things. We think a monumental goal like creating a remarkable life must require massive, relentless action. It doesn't. Forget the towering plan and don't focus on your entire life. Begin with one day. Start with the easiest and most practical things you can do, and trust that over time the cumulative results will make a difference. You are putting in place the disciplines and actions that will yield a life you will be excited to live. Forget extravagance and get down to the basics.

If you want to travel to Paris, then learn about the city, the sights, the people, and the history. Dive into the logistics. Start looking up flights and hotels. Figure out where you want to stay and the parts of the city you want to avoid. Tell people you are planning on visiting Paris. If they've been, ask them what they liked most and least, and ask for recommendations.

Start planning your daily itinerary. Even if your trip is years away, the sheer process of planning the details will make the trip even more real. By researching it, and talking about it, you'll notice news stories about Paris, you'll overhear people talking about their recent trip to the City of Lights.

Once the idea is real and visceral, it will be easier to move from idea to action. You'll tally up the cost of the trip you have planned. You'll calculate the trade-offs you must make to pay for it. Maybe you'll work overtime or save more. You'll explore all the options, because the once-vague trip to Paris is now palpable and tangible. All you have to do is pick a date and put your plan into action. Too often we wait to plan until we've committed to a date. Reverse the order. Plan as if you were going in a month. Action generates more action. Repeated actions create momentum, and momentum is hard to stop. Let it move you from idea to reality.

Part of planning your perfect life involved listing the people you'd like to meet. There are practical steps you can take. If you want to meet a particular author, look for their book signings and attend. Want to meet a musician? Go to their shows. Write them a letter. Follow the people you want to meet on social media. Tell people about the individuals you'd like to meet. Someone may surprise you and tell you they can introduce you.

There is no guarantee you will meet the people you want to meet, but like everything else, you will find more success when you take action and try. Put it out there. Let people know the details of the life you want to live. It may not happen like you imagined, but some things that happen will surprise you.

Every year I set goals for the year, and I always include a list of people I'd like to meet. It's random and I know there are no guarantees that I will meet everyone or anyone on the list. But I find unexpected opportunities arise repeatedly that have allowed me the chance to meet people whose names I put on my list.

Last year, a few of the names on my "People I'd Like to Meet" list were James Clear, Scott Harrison, and Zachary Levi. James is the author of *Atomic Habits*. Scott is the founder of a nonprofit called charity: water and author of *Thirst*. Zachary Levi is an actor. He was the lead character of the television show *Chuck* and played the starring role in the superhero movie *Shazam!*. I put James and Scott on my list after reading their excellent books. The show *Chuck* was a family favorite for me and my kids, and a show we rewatch regularly. All three are just random people I thought would be fun to meet.

In March 2019, someone asked me to speak at an event on innovation. I created and delivered a session I called The Innovation of You. That talk became the starting point for this book. I incorporated some of James Clear's ideas on habits. I recommended the book to everyone in the audience. I had already read *Atomic Habits* twice in the first three months of the year. I told many people about James Clear and his down-to-earth approach to habit-setting.

Two months later I delivered The Innovation of You again. The people arranging the event knew I'd been recommending *Atomic Habits* and asked if I would like to have James join me to talk about habits. A few weeks later I got to meet James and take the stage with him. Six months prior, I hadn't heard of James Clear. Then I read his book, talked to hundreds of people about it, and added his name to my "People I'd Like to Meet" list. Things have a way of working out. But I would not have met James had I not talked so much about *Atomic Habits*.

I saw Scott Harrison's book, *Thirst*, featured in a display at the Amazon bookstore. The customer rating was 4.9, a much higher rating than most books receive. The book is about Scott's journey from nightclub promoter to founder of a nonprofit organization bringing clean water to people throughout the world with no access to clean water. I bought the book and read it that night.

Scott's story is captivating, and the work of charity: water is so vital. I finished the book on a flight to Ireland. The guy sitting next to me asked if I enjoyed it. I gave him the book and told him he should read it. I've purchased several copies of *Thirst* and keep giving them away. When I was adding names to my people list, Scott Harrison came to mind in an instant.

Scott lives in New York. I live in California. I looked at events where he might be speaking. I checked out charity: water's event schedule. There wasn't anything I could find that would provide an opportunity to meet Scott. But I work for LinkedIn, the world's largest professional network. If I couldn't meet him in person, I thought I could connect with him on LinkedIn. I sent him a note and an invitation to connect, and Scott graciously replied and accepted. I'd still like to have coffee with Scott someday, but I was happy to connect with him and let him know how much I appreciated his book and the work he's doing. It's progress.

Sometimes things happen because you seek them out. Other times they just happen. Such was the case with Zachary Levi. Alan Smyth is a longtime friend of mine. He is the executive director of a nonprofit organization called Saving Innocence that rescues kids and young adults from sex trafficking. He invited me to attend a fundraising gala for Saving Innocence and the important work they do, and Vicky and I went.

The gala was in Hollywood. We flew down the night before, took in the sights, then headed to the Saving Innocence gala. Vicky was checking us in, and I went to look for Alan. As I scanned the sea of faces in the ballroom, I didn't see Alan, but I saw Zachary Levi. He was standing twenty feet away, by himself. I walked over and introduced myself, then told him how much I enjoyed *Chuck*. We stood in the middle of hundreds of people and had a friendly conversation. He was gracious and humble, even taking a selfie of the two of us with my phone.

The encounters didn't change my life. But they added color and excitement to my story. Moments make up our lives. Memorable moments make them remarkable. Sometimes we fool ourselves into thinking only the significant events affect our story. But it's actually the cumulative effect of every moment, significant and small, that makes a difference. As Annie Dillard says in *The Writing Life*, "How we spend our days is, of course, how we spend our lives."

You probably won't meet every person whose name you put on your list, but you may find that fortuitous events conspire to provide you with some entertaining encounters. Have some fun with it. Who would you like to meet?

Whether it's the places you want to go, the people you want to meet, or the adventures you'd like to experience, begin with simple steps. Start small. Look for the practical ways you can pursue your goals, whether it's a LinkedIn connection or a letter. Keep taking practical steps and see what happens. You may be surprised by the people you meet and the places you'll go.

11

A NEW POINT OF VIEW

In his bestselling memoir, *Tuesdays with Morrie*, Mitch Albom shares the story of his relationship with Morrie Schwartz, his favorite college professor. Despite their intentions, Mitch and Morrie lose touch after Mitch graduates. Twenty years later, Mitch sees Morrie being interviewed on *Nightline* and hears that his professor is dying of ALS, Lou Gehrig's disease.

Mitch visits Morrie, and they rekindle their relationship. They meet every Tuesday for the last months of Morrie's life, and Mitch gets the privilege of learning again from his professor. The lessons are about love and loss, friendship and death, and how important it is to treasure life and the people with whom you share it.

Morrie is frail, confined to his house, but even in this he has wisdom to share with Mitch: "[Morrie] nodded toward the window with the sunshine streaming in. 'You see that? You can go out there, outside, anytime. You can run up and down the block and go crazy. I can't do that. I can't go out. I can't run. I can't be out there without fear of getting sick. But you know what? I *appreciate* that window more than you do.'"[1] Morrie had mastered the art of perspective and appreciation.

You don't have to go far to get started creating the life you want. The best place to begin is where you are, in this moment. Aesop said, "Gratitude turns what we have into enough." Sometimes it's helpful when somebody reminds you how good your life already is.

Jeff and I went to high school together. He was the proverbial social butterfly, loved being in the middle of the action, was voted the biggest flirt, and is the most active person on Facebook I know. Vicky and I went to Maui last year. We were enjoying fabulous food, spectacular sunsets, and beautiful beaches. She posted a few pictures from our day together, and I had to laugh when I saw a reply from Jeff. He wrote, "Kevin. You are not allowed to ask for anything more."

I could almost hear him saying, *You've reached your limit. You are beyond lucky. You have more than enough.* I loved his perspective. Too often we focus on what we don't have, the things we want, all that's missing. But we don't need more. We have enough already. We can improve our life in an instant if we learn to appreciate what we already have.

In August 1911, a handyman named Vincenzo Peruggia walked into the Louvre Museum in Paris, removed a frame from the wall, and walked out with the painting tucked under his arm. No one even noticed the painting was missing for over twenty-four hours.

The Italians call the painting *La Gioconda*, the French *La Joconde*. Most of the world knows her as the *Mona Lisa*. Regardless of what you call her, she is a priceless masterpiece and considered the most famous painting in the world. But that wasn't always the case.

Although renowned master Leonardo da Vinci painted the *Mona Lisa*, it wasn't a well-known painting. Most people had never heard of the *Mona Lisa*. People weren't lining up to see it. But that changed when word got out that the painting was missing.

The police arrived, and an investigation began. They handed out thousands of leaflets, all bearing the image of *Mona Lisa*, each offering a reward for her return. The missing painting made headlines. Word spread. Soon, people were showing up in droves, lining up just to see the space on the wall where the *Mona Lisa* once hung.

The investigation went on for over two years, and with each break in the case, more headlines created more interest in the painting. The once-obscure work of art that hung unguarded on a wall in the Louvre was now the most recognizable painting in the world.[2] Why is it we so rarely appreciate the amazing things in our lives when they are right in front of us and only realize how special they are once they're gone?

Nothing changed to make the *Mona Lisa* more appealing. The allure was that she went missing. Today, over nine million people visit the Louvre each year. Almost all of them line up to see this most famous painting protected behind bulletproof glass and watched by a guard dedicated to protecting the *Mona Lisa* alone.

Sometimes we don't appreciate what we have until it's too late. When my life almost ended, I came away with a much deeper appreciation for what I already had. I had wonderful people in my life and so much to be thankful for, but it meant I needed to pay more attention to the beauty right in front of me.

There is no shortage of things for us to appreciate. We are surrounded by awe-inspiring beauty. Majestic mountain ranges and redwoods that reach into the sky, so impressive that photographs cannot capture the wonder. The artistry of the clouds and the ocean, the birds that fly overhead. There is so much to marvel at. If you master the art of appreciating the overlooked and unappreciated blessings in your life, you will add to the joy you experience. It's not the lack of wonderful things to see, only the effort it takes to appreciate them.

If you aren't happy with the life you are living, another point of view might help you realize it's better than you think it is. Depending on how we interpret our circumstances, we can see life as an adventure or an ordeal. Henry David Thoreau noted, "The question is not what you look at, but what you see." If you see only what's wrong with your life, you will live a miserable one. But without changing a single aspect of your life, you can look deeper and realize how good you already have it. If your life isn't everything you want it to be, what might you not be seeing?

You wake up in the morning, groggy and slow. You stretch

your still-tired body, shake off the cobwebs of sleep, and summon the courage to get out of bed. You open your eyes to get on with the day. But instead of seeing your usual sleep-induced, blurry-eyed version of the morning, you see nothing. Your world remains in darkness. You rub your eyes and blink a few times to clear the sleep away. Still nothing. Without warning, your world is now one of shadows forever.

How much would you miss your sight if you lost it forever? Pause for a moment and imagine your life without sight from this moment forward. What would you miss seeing most? The eyes of your child? Your smiling spouse? The sky awash in brilliant color by the setting sun? We don't always appreciate things until they're gone. When was the last time you woke up and just appreciated the fact that you can still see?

For the thirty-nine million blind people in the world, that's not something they get to experience.[3] They wake up in darkness every day. If we could keep in mind how precious a gift our sight is, maybe we would be more intentional about looking at the world, and not just looking, but seeing. The beauty, the people, the colors. We might wonder and stand rapt in awe. Wouldn't life be so much better if we did?

Helen Keller was blind since childhood. She wrote about the joy she experienced through touch. Smooth and rough textures of leaves and trees. The symmetry and shape of everyday objects, the velvety feel of a flower. The quiver of a bird sitting on a nearby branch. She imagined how much more she could enjoy the beauty of the world if she could see, but then noted, "Those who have eyes apparently see little. The panorama of color and action which fills the world is taken for granted. . . . it is a great pity that in the world of light the gift of sight is used only as a mere convenience rather than as a means of adding fullness to life."[4] Are you one of those who sees very little?

The blessings we take for granted extend far beyond seeing the world in which we live. You reach to open the door in front of you, only your arms don't respond. Despite your effort and desire to grab the doorknob and turn it, your arms ignore your instructions. Hundreds, if not thousands, of times each day we pick things up. We touch and feel and hold. A pen to write, a fork to eat. Lifting a cup of coffee, turning on a faucet, holding a baby. But what if your arms hung unresponsive by your side, no longer able to move, no longer capable of accomplishing the multitude of tasks you do daily without thought or effort?

On May 27, 1995, Hollywood actor Christopher Reeve, best known for his role as Superman, was thrown from a horse while riding. He landed headfirst on the ground, crushing his first and second vertebrae. The forty-two-year-old, handsome leading man became paralyzed from the neck down. He would spend the rest of his life in a wheelchair, unable to breathe without the help of a ventilator.[5] In an instance, everything changed.

In the United States alone, there are 5.4 million paralyzed people.[6] That's 1 in 50 people. Worldwide, about 1 billion people live with some form of disability.[7] For anyone who wakes up in the morning with the ability to get out of bed on their own and go about their day with no need for a wheelchair, this should be reason to celebrate.

Your life is better than you realize it is. If you can see the world around you and walk where you want to go, you should be thankful. And if you can hear? Then you should add that to the list of things to appreciate. There are 466 million people in the world with disabling hearing loss.[8] The singing birds, the sound of laughter, the conversations that happen throughout your day? All affected. How different would your life be if you were deaf?

We forget to appreciate the wonder of our everyday blessings. If you want perspective on how blessed you are, go on the internet and watch a few videos of deaf people hearing sound for the first time after getting cochlear implants. The moment they hear sound, it overwhelms them with joy.

There is a beautiful moment with a deaf woman named Andrea Diaz, who had cochlear devices implanted. In the video we are in the doctor's office. When the audiologist turns on the cochlear implants, Andrea will hear for the first time. She is there with her boyfriend, whose voice she has never heard. They turn the implants on and, as expected, Andrea is overjoyed as she takes in the surrounding sounds. Then it gets even better. Her boyfriend gets down on one knee, takes out a ring, and proposes. He says, "I wanted to make this one of the first things you hear . . ." and then he asks Andrea to marry him.[9] To see the joy experienced as a deaf person receives the gift of hearing will impress on us the wonderful gift of hearing we already have.

Sometimes it's helpful to see others appreciating the things we have. They remind us of the blessings we take for granted. Do you get annoyed with your family? Go watch some videos of kids hearing they are getting adopted. It's a wonderful reminder of how people long for a family when they don't have one. Don't like your job? It's better than being unemployed. You may not be living in the home of your dreams, but it would be a castle to the homeless person on the street. You and I cry over spilled champagne, while 790 million people lack access to clean water. We hate cleaning the bathroom, but 1.8 billion people don't have access to adequate sanitation.[10] We rarely stop to appreciate that we have access to a bathroom and clean water, but we might if we realized about 485,000 people die every year of diseases from contaminated water.[11] We have it so good without even knowing it.

When you were thinking about your perfect life, did you think to include being able to see and hear? Did you include being able to walk and smell and taste? Did your perfect life include having access to clean drinking water and sanitation? We take for granted the essential but most meaningful parts of life. If we can learn to appreciate the everyday blessings we already have, we may find we are closer to living the life we want to live than we realized.

12

WHAT'S NOT WRONG

I f we can improve life with something as simple as appreciating what we already have, why don't we? Because we are fantastic at finding fault, figuring out every-thing that's wrong with the world and the people in it. We focus so much on the flaws that we overlook what's good and right. We need to get better at noticing what's not wrong if we are to enjoy life to its fullest.

You wake up in the morning, and you've got a splitting headache. It's pervasive and distracting. All you think about is how your head is pounding. You take some Tylenol and push through the day, the medicine goes to work, and your headache fades away. But more often than not, you wake up and you don't have a headache. You get up and shower, and the day begins. This is the norm. Very few days include the headache. But do you ever get up and appreciate that you don't have a headache? How often do we stop and take stock of all that's *not* wrong?

It's not to say that troubling times and difficult circumstances will not affect us, but we give too much attention to the negative. We obsess over slight imperfections while ignoring the multitude of blessings. If we are intentional about looking for all that's going well, we'd soon realize we have much to celebrate.

Make a list of twenty things that are *not* wrong in your life now. Get some paper or open your computer and start writing. It's good to remind yourself of what we so often forget. We need to retrain ourselves to see what's right instead of noticing all that's wrong. What if you added five things to your list every day? What if you read over the list of things going right in your life once a week? It's a simple action, but it would go a long way toward keeping the enjoyable things in our life at the forefront of our minds rather than forgotten and ignored.

Did you make your list of twenty things that are *not* wrong in your life? It was a simple thing to do, but it doesn't matter how simple something is if you don't take the time to do it. Improving your life doesn't have to be a massive transformation or change; it could be the cumulative effect of doing simple things. You can improve your life by remembering the overlooked blessings you already have in your life. Don't skip doing the work. Make your list of twenty things. If you did, add another twenty things to your list. You may find yourself even more grateful and happy for the life you already have.

It takes effort to stop what you are doing to make a list. We have every good intention of doing it later, but with every passing second you don't act, the likelihood of you ever following through diminishes. Delayed action translates to no action. It's the same for me. As I write about making a list, it's inconvenient to pause and do what I'm asking you to do. Talk is cheap, so I am making my list now.

Things that are not wrong in my life:

1. I have a wonderful wife who loves me.
2. Aidan, Brendan, and Kylie (my kids) are healthy.
3. The sun is shining.
4. My car started this morning and got me to work without issue.
5. I didn't get in an accident, get a flat tire, or miss every green light.
6. I got to see my parents yesterday. I'm fortunate they are both still alive.
7. I have a job. Not everyone is as lucky.
8. I work with intelligent people at a company that does meaningful work.
9. I have a house that provides a clean, dry place to sleep.
10. War is not raging in my city.
11. I have access to all the food I need.
12. I have an unlimited supply of clean water. Filtered water, sparkling water, bottled water.
13. I have clean clothes to wear.
14. I get to enjoy playing the piano whenever I want.
15. I have easy access to information in an instant.
16. I have thousands and thousands of pictures reminding me of fantastic memories with my family.
17. Vicky and I are going to Hawaii in a week.

18. The stock market is down huge today. But I'm fortunate enough to have money available to invest in the stock market. Not everyone does.
19. I'm listening to beautiful classical music as I write.
20. I am vertical and conscious, something too often taken for granted. It means I'm alive.

Any day you wake up alive is a gift not experienced by everyone. As I'm writing this, I hear news reports that NBA star Kobe Bryant, along with one of his four daughters, died in a helicopter crash this morning. He was forty-one years old and leaves behind Vanessa, his wife of nineteen years, and three daughters. Take the time to remind yourself of what's good about your life.

Someone we can all learn from in this area is Johnny Jones. There's a lot he could complain about, but he has learned to focus on what's *not* wrong in his life.

Staff Sergeant Joey Jones

Johnny "Joey" Jones was a typical American kid. He grew up in Georgia, loved playing football, and after high school, he joined the Marines. Johnny got deployed to Afghanistan as an explosive ordnance disposal technician, meaning his job was to find and defuse bombs.

On a sweltering August day in 2010, Johnny and two additional bomb technicians were working their way through small alleyways and collapsed buildings looking for signs of any explosive devices. In the previous five days, they had already cleared fifty IEDs, improvised explosive devices. They found a stash of unassembled bomb parts hidden under some old boxes and tires and cleared them away. Tired and hot, Johnny leaned against a wall to rest for a few moments. When he got up to continue his search for more explosives, he took a step away from the wall and stepped on an IED.[1]

The bomb detonated, and it blew Jones and his fellow soldiers thirty feet in the explosion. Corporal Daniel Greer would die from his wounds. The blast wounded Staff Sergeant Eric Chir with shrapnel. Johnny Jones lost both his legs and suffered severe damage to both his arms.

Jones had a tough time in the hospital. He felt helpless, realizing he needed to relearn even the most basic life skills. The many surgeries exhausted Jones, and he found himself second-guessing all that had happened. *If only I'd stepped left instead of right. If only . . .* But Jones soon decided that life was for the living, and as long as he was alive, he would make the most of his life. He decided he would have a positive attitude and use his energy to help others overcome adversity.

Johnny Jones exemplifies someone who focuses on what's right and not on what's wrong. He loves to say, "People ask how I stay so positive after losing my legs. I simply ask how they stay so negative with theirs."[2]

Choosing to focus on what's not wrong does not suggest you ignore the difficulties or deny they exist. It means despite the reality of life's challenges and imperfections, there is still so much that we can appreciate if we choose to. Be someone who learns to see what's right about life. It takes effort. We excel at finding the negatives and flaws. Be different. It will make a world of difference in your life.

13

IS IT WORTH IT?

M aybe you are thinking, *This all seems like a lot of work —dreaming big, designing life, goals, giving. Is it worth it?* Everyone must determine whether something is important to them, but a life lived well rises to the level of worthwhile for me. Only you can decide what is worth your time and energy. The question is not whether it's worth the effort to create an extraordinary life, it's understanding the alternative.

Jim Rohn noted, "We must all suffer from one of two pains; the pain of discipline or the pain of regret. The difference is discipline weighs ounces while regret weighs tons." Yes, it takes effort to live an extraordinary life. But the pain of discipline required to live an extraordinary life is nothing compared to the pain of regret so many people experience at the end of their life if they didn't try.

Living life takes effort whether you make it remarkable or one of mediocrity. We are all creating something with our lives. What are you creating with yours? Are you focusing your actions and energy to create the life you want or just going through the motions, passing days with no particular destination in mind? Since life requires effort either way, why not do all you can with your one wild and precious life?

Understanding what you want to do with your life, and who you want to become, is the foundation for creating the life you want to live. Dreaming big helps you identify the specifics. It's equally important to explore the reasons for the things you want to do. If your reasons are big enough, they will pull you forward and compel you to action, and action is the essential ingredient to moving your dreams from ideas to reality. We are all living for something. What is your *something*, your *why*, that makes it all worthwhile? To live the life you want to live, you must understand your purpose.

PART III

FINDING YOUR PURPOSE

Definiteness of purpose is the starting point of all achievement.

—W. Clement Stone

14

PURPOSE DEFINED

W hat is the purpose of your life? I've asked hundreds of people this question, and most don't have an answer. Perhaps it's because we lack clarity on what we mean by *purpose*.

What is the purpose of life?

- The Dalai Lama believes, "The very purpose of life is to be happy."
- Robert F. Kennedy asserted, "The purpose of life is to contribute in some way to making things better."
- Eleanor Roosevelt said, "The purpose of life, after all, is to live it, to taste experience to the utmost, to reach out eagerly and without fear for newer and richer experience."

Three great minds with three different definitions, maybe some truth in each. Just as each of us designs and creates the life we want to live, we determine how we define purpose for ourselves. There's no shortage of resources available to help you.

Head to the bookstore and you will find volumes of books on the subject of purpose. Thousands of resources are available to help you lead with purpose, parent with purpose, work with purpose. You can discover your path to purpose, the road to purpose, and the possibilities of purpose. And why not? Purpose drives the big questions of life. Why do I exist? What is the meaning of my life? Why am I here? Of all the questions you will answer in the course of your life, these rise near the top of the list.

Merriam-Webster defines *purpose* as:
1. the reason for which something exists
2. an intended or desired result; end; aim; goal
3. determination; resoluteness

Synonyms for *purpose* include:
1. goal
2. commitment
3. motivation
4. single-mindedness
5. resolve

A remarkable life encompasses all these words and definitions. Our purpose includes our goals and commitments. It depends on our motivation and resolve. You can live a life of purpose with single-mindedness and determination. It's not accidental, but on purpose, intentional. The purpose of life is the reason we exist.

It all boils down to one thing. We want our lives to mean

something. After living sixty or seventy or eighty years, we want to believe that all the effort we exerted throughout our lives was meaningful. We want to know that the world is better because we were in it. Our purpose is the rationale for all we've done in pursuit of meaning.

When you think about your life, designing it and living it to the fullest, you will need to be single-minded in your goal to live a life with no regret, intentional about taking the actions necessary to bring your dreams to reality, and resolved to push past the obstacles of life that will inevitably arise. If your purpose is compelling enough, you will stay the course and ensure you don't end your life with the agony of an untold story still inside you.

You will encounter difficulties as you pursue the life you want. A remarkable life is impossible without purpose. If we want our lives to matter, it requires intentionality, despite the resistance. That's where purpose enters the equation. French philosopher Michel de Montaigne wrote, "The soul which has no fixed purpose in life is lost; to be everywhere is to be nowhere." Purpose moves us from lost to found, from directionless to destination.

Determining your purpose is deciding where you want to be. It brings clarity on how you should spend your time. It helps you stay focused on what is important and helpful in allowing you to live the life you want to live. Purpose provides direction so you avoid confusion on which way you should go. It's the engine that drives you to take the actions that will help you reach your goals. The stronger your purpose, the more success you will have.

Defining your perfect life tells you what you want from life, but understanding your purpose tells you why. Purpose provides the pressure test of our plans. It requires us to question our actions if they don't align with our purpose. If your purpose is lacking, your plans will crumble, and if your plans crumble, you won't live the life you want to live. Lives without purpose end with regret. To move from designing life to living it, we need to better understand the many ways purpose will play its part.

15

SINGLE-MINDED PURPOSE

Growing up, I thought someone's life purpose was a preordained pursuit for them to discover, a person's particular contribution to the world for them to fulfill. With that definition, there is tremendous gravity when determining our purpose in life. Imagine the regret you would feel to realize on your deathbed you pursued the wrong life purpose and never fulfilled your contribution to the world. I had trouble figuring out what my major in college would be, let alone determining the purpose of my life. So I looked to those who figured it out to see what I could learn. Andrew Carnegie was the first person who came to mind. His life was a success, and his single-minded purpose seemed to be the reason.

The Star-Spangled Scotsman

Carnegie was born in Scotland in 1835. His parents were

weavers who didn't have a lot of money. When Andrew was twelve years old, he and his parents moved to Pennsylvania in pursuit of a better life. At thirteen, Carnegie began working in a cotton factory in Pittsburgh, six days a week, twelve hours a day, for the paltry sum of $1.20 per week in wages. Carnegie's life is one of the great rags-to-riches stories. From his humble, hardworking beginnings, he invested his savings in railroads and oil derricks. He worked as a bond salesman and then poured his energy into building the Carnegie Steel Company. When he sold his steel business to J. P. Morgan, Andrew Carnegie became the richest person in America.[1]

What's amazing about Carnegie was the single-minded purpose he laid out for himself when he was a young man. Carnegie set a two-part goal for himself that would guide his actions throughout his life. He committed to make as much money as possible during the first half of his life. And the second half, he committed to giving it away.[2] With that single-minded purpose, Carnegie rose from poverty to prosperity. True to his purpose, he followed through on the second half of his goal. Carnegie spent the last half of his life focused on philanthropy, investing heavily in education to allow others the opportunity to improve their life circumstances. He set up the public library system, built Carnegie Hall to celebrate the arts, established the Carnegie Endowment for International Peace, and constructed Carnegie Mellon University and the Carnegie Museums of Pittsburgh.[3]

Carnegie appreciated that people had helped him along the way. When he worked at the factory, his boss gave him and the other boys access to his personal library. The knowledge Carnegie learned in those books helped him change the course of his life. His philanthropic efforts focused on libraries because he wanted to afford underprivileged people access to the knowledge that could help them help themselves. What's amazing about Carnegie is that he determined his life's purpose early and stayed with it the rest of his life. He was a success beyond anyone's expectations. His single-minded purpose helped him rise from poverty to the richest person in America and provided him the means to give back to society through generous philanthropy.

Raising Champions

Richard Williams is someone else who had clarity on his single-minded purpose in life. Williams grew up in Shreveport, Louisiana, one of five children. His mother was a former sharecropper and his father was mostly absent. Poverty and abuse marked his childhood. He was no stranger to trouble. He began stealing when he was eight years old, selling what he stole to provide for his family. Growing up in the South, Williams lived in a time of deep racial tension. He experienced the turmoil firsthand when Ku Klux Klan members harassed and beat him.

When Williams was almost forty years old, he was flipping through the television channels and stopped on the awards ceremony for the French Open, a tennis tournament held in Paris every year. Williams wasn't a tennis player and didn't have any interest in the sport, but it shocked him to find out that the winner earned $40,000. He decided at that moment that he would have two kids and that he would turn them into tennis stars.[4]

Richard wrote a seventy-eight-page plan detailing how he

would accomplish this challenging feat for his unborn children. Step one was for Richard to learn how to play tennis. He taught himself by watching instructional videos and then found a mentor in a man he called Old Whiskey, which seemed fitting since he paid the man in pints of booze.[5]

Williams and his wife, Oracene, had two daughters, Venus and Serena. Before they were in kindergarten, Richard set to work teaching them how to play tennis. Richard moved his family to Compton, California, an area renowned for crime, gangs, and drugs. Williams had studied the lives of people he admired, like Muhammad Ali and Malcolm X, and believed that the toughness developed in the ghetto was an asset. Moving to the rough neighborhoods in Compton was part of his plan to create champions.

Venus and Serena learned to play tennis on the public tennis courts of Compton. The poor condition of the courts wasn't the only issue affecting their training, though. Local drug dealers liked to deal their drugs from the tennis courts. Richard tried to negotiate to have them leave so the girls could practice. This led to many altercations between gang members and Richard. He suffered broken bones and knocked-out teeth, but after two years of persistence, the gang members yielded and the girls could use the tennis courts to practice.

Richard executed his seventy-eight-page plan, working relentlessly with his two daughters. And it paid off better than anyone could have imagined. His daughter Venus turned pro at fourteen. Within three years she broke into the top fifty players in the world. Six years after turning pro, Venus won her first Grand Slam singles title, Wimbledon.

That same year she won the US Open and a gold medal in the Olympics. During her career she won seven Grand Slam singles titles, fourteen doubles titles with her sister, and another two mixed doubles titles with her partner Justin Gimelstob. She earned more than $41 million in prize money, placing her second on the all-time earnings list for female tennis players.[6]

But remember, Richard's plan was to raise two champions. It's hard to imagine topping the accomplishments of Venus, but somehow Serena did. She turned pro at fourteen, just like her sister. Serena won twenty-three Grand Slam singles titles, the fourteen doubles titles with Venus, and another two with mixed doubles partner Max Mirnyi. Serena earned a staggering $92 million in prize money during her career, more than any woman in history.[7]

There is power in having a clear, single-minded purpose. It guides your actions and drives you in a very specific direction. Richard Williams showed how strong a single-minded purpose can be, starting from the very bottom, with no knowledge or experience, then creating a plan for his unborn children to conquer the world of tennis. What might you accomplish if you were to pursue your purpose, single-mindedly, with everything you have?

While you are imagining the significant heights you can scale with your single-minded purpose, keep in mind that everything has a cost and a price to pay. When you say yes to a single-minded purpose, it means you need to say no to many other opportunities. Richard invested significant amounts of money to fund his plan of raising champions. He moved the family to Compton so the hardship of living in a tough town would strengthen Venus and Serena. Something he didn't expect was losing a child.

Yetunde was the oldest half sister of Venus and Serena. She and her boyfriend were sitting in a parked SUV in a south Compton neighborhood. Members of the Crips street gang mistakenly thought the SUV belonged to rival gang members. They opened fired on the SUV, shooting Yetunde in the head. She died a short while after arriving at the hospital.[8]

Beyond the tragic and unexpected death of Yetunde, there were other challenges in raising champions. Richard knew that Venus and Serena were likely to encounter racism in the predominantly white, wealthy game of tennis. To make sure the emotional toll would not derail his plan, Richard paid kids from the neighborhood to come to the tennis courts while Venus and Serena were practicing to distract them by any means possible. They yelled insults and racial slurs at the girls while they practiced, as Richard reminded them to focus on the game and not the distractions. The ability to tune out the noise and insults became a powerful weapon in the girls' arsenal.

Richard took other steps to ensure his plan stayed on course. He deemed boyfriends and babies to be deadly enemy number one, knowing a romantic relationship could introduce all kinds of unwanted turmoil for the girls. Richard forbade the girls to date, and he even tore the heads off Venus and Serena's dolls so as not to encourage any thoughts of motherhood.

Richard's single-minded purpose was to raise two tennis champions. He sacrificed and paid the price required to create champions, and the results are undeniable. Like Carnegie before him, Richard Williams succeeded far beyond anyone's wildest dreams. Both men had deep convictions, which they backed up with consistent and bold actions. The discipline they both exhibited is staggering, and yet that's not the part of their stories that stands out for me. It's that both had such clarity, a single-minded purpose. I think that's rare.

16

FROM ONE TO MANY

A s I was growing up, I found it overwhelming to think about my purpose in life. It was such a big decision. Nothing seemed to rise to the level of worthiness that would hold the title of *my life's purpose*. But I know I'm not alone. In fact, I would say very few people have clarity on their life's purpose to the degree Andrew Carnegie and Richard Williams did.

We have a few general ideas, high level and unspecific: *make the world a better place. Be a good person.* But these lack the clarity and specificity of someone pursuing a passion they feel they were born to pursue. Some people know their life's purpose, but most do not. We can admire those who do, but if you don't, that's okay. I don't think we need to know. It would serve us better to make the mental shift from trying to figure out life's one purpose to exploring life's many purposes.

Your purpose doesn't remain static through the many seasons of your life. What I knew about life, and how I could live it, was far different in my twenties than it is today. As we grow, our desires and resources change, our passions shift. So does the purpose of our life. When we build something up as *the one*, it can be paralyzing. While searching for our one true love, we miss out on relationships with other amazing people. While we ponder the universe and life's deeper meaning, it can tempt us to remain on the sidelines of commitment, afraid of pursuing the wrong purpose. So we wait. Don't! Not if you want to live an extraordinary life.

Pour your passions into what excites you today. Pick a purpose, any purpose, and give it your time, energy, and talent. Here's the wonderful news. If six months from now you stumble onto your life's *true* purpose, then let go of the old one and upgrade to the new. Nothing lost. You will have contributed to something for a season of life, and now you will contribute to something else. Too many people sit inactive, giving their time and energy to nothing because they aren't sure if it's their one purpose in life. Stop waiting. Pick a purpose and pursue it.

Not sure what to pick? Spend some time thinking about the possibilities. Make a list of ten purposes you might have over the course of your life. Finding purpose requires action. Designing an extraordinary life will take effort. Don't skip the work or you won't get the results. What are ten purposes you could have in your life?

As I look back on the different seasons of my life, I can see several distinct purposes I was pursuing. As my life changed, so did my passions and pursuits. My purpose varied in each of those seasons, but each had meaning and contributed to the overall story of my life.

I found purpose in being a husband and father, writing

songs and performing, and teaching. I had seasons of purpose as a basketball coach and diving coach. I had years of purpose working with high school students as a volunteer with Young Life. I continue to find purpose supporting organizations doing meaningful work and helping people early in their career succeed. And I'm looking to add purpose to my life as a writer. What roles will you play, and how can you find meaning in them?

Purpose through Music. In my twenties, I focused my energy on being a musician. I learned to play a variety of instruments and wrote hundreds of songs. I wrote about the challenges, questions, and disappointments of life. When I played, I shared the life stories that inspired my songs. People often told me how the music affected them and helped them to realize they weren't alone in their struggles. They thanked me for encouraging them to persevere despite the difficulties. Twenty-five years later, I still get notes from people saying how much my music meant to them.

A friend sent me a magazine article that included an interview of a recording artist named Jonah Werner. In the interview Jonah said, "When Kevin sang, it connected with my heart in a way nothing ever had."[1] Jonah is now reaching audiences with his own stories through music. It's important to remember, we never know how our actions are affecting others. I wasn't good enough or persistent enough to make a living with music, but I could still affect people and make a difference with my music. Of my many life purposes, I appreciate that music was a season of purpose for me.

Purpose as a Father. I am blessed with three kids, Aidan, Brendan, and Kylie. At the time of my transplant they were twelve, ten, and seven years old. Watching them grow up has been one of the most meaningful parts of the past twelve years. With a second chance to live a remarkable life, I wanted to make sure we created a lifetime of memories together. I wanted to be intentional about creating experiences they would remember.

Every year we go on our Delaney Family Adventure. The goal of our DFAs is to go somewhere we've never been and to do things we've never done. The trips are about creating memories, collecting experiences, and spending time together. The DFAs are also a chance for me to remind them how much I love them, and how grateful I am for every extra day I've been able to spend with them. Being a father has provided me with countless moments of purpose and greater meaning in life.

Purpose through Appreciation. Being a father has also helped me appreciate my own parents so much more. As a kid, you can't comprehend the sacrifices your parents make to provide for you. We are too busy complaining about all we don't have instead of appreciating what we're given. As I've grown older and had kids of my own, I look back with a much deeper appreciation for all that my parents did for me.

My parents arrived in America with nothing. They both worked hard to create an enjoyable life for our family. By the time I was in high school, my dad was working in a corporate job as a purchasing manager. I did not understand what that meant. But every night I saw him prepare for work the next day, hanging a pressed shirt on the back of a chair in the kitchen, and laying out his cigarettes and pen on the table.

He got up early every day and went to work and returned before dinner in the evening. I never heard him complain about his job once. When I was in college trying to figure out what I wanted to do with my life, I looked at my dad's routine and was certain I never wanted to do something so mundane and repetitive. Decades into my career, I appreciate more than ever the example of his work ethic and attitude in doing what he needed to do to provide. I am inspired by my dad's consistency over the decades.

I'm fortunate that both of my parents are still alive. They provided me with everything I needed growing up and continue to be unconditional in their support. It's a new season of life and one where I can give back. There is purpose in appreciating all they've done for me, and purpose in helping take care of their needs.

Dostoyevsky said, "The mystery of human existence lies not in just staying alive, but in finding something to live for." Purpose helps you find your something. In the next section we will explore several ways to find more purpose: moments of purpose, giving wings to someone else's purpose, personal purpose, opportunistic purpose, and purpose at work.

17

MOMENTS OF PURPOSE

When you make the shift from thinking about your one purpose in life to your many purposes, doors of opportunity will open. We all want lives filled with meaning, and we can find more meaning through purpose. The more ways we can interject purpose into our days, the more meaning we will have in life.

By broadening our understanding of how and where we can find purpose, we can increase the possibilities of impact. It doesn't require a lifetime of effort, or even a season. You can create purpose in a single moment, and it can affect people for the rest of their lives.

Superman and the Proctologist

Christopher Reeve and Robin Williams met at The Juilliard School. They started as roommates and became close friends. They both became major Hollywood stars, Robin getting his break on the television series *Mork & Mindy* and Christopher with his starring role in the movie *Superman*. Their friendship lasted the rest of their lives.[1]

When a horseback riding accident left Reeve paralyzed, he faced a delicate surgery to reattach his spine to his skull. Doctors gave him a 50 percent chance of surviving the surgery. Reeve became depressed and suicidal thinking about life as a quadriplegic. His nights were agonizing. He was anxious and alone, waiting for the pending surgery that might end his life.

Reeve was in his hospital room when the door opened and a doctor in full scrubs rushed into the room. The doctor spoke in a heavy Russian accent. He explained to Reeve that he was a proctologist and that he needed to do a rectal exam right away. Reeve couldn't understand why he would need a proctologist, then realized that the energetic Russian doctor was not a doctor at all, but his dear friend Robin Williams. He couldn't help but laugh. Reeve said, "For the first time since the accident, I laughed. My old friend had helped me know that somehow I was going to be okay. . . . I knew then: if I could laugh, I could live."[2]

One minute Reeve was alone and depressed in a hospital room; the next, he was laughing and optimistic about the future. In a moment Robin reminded his friend that life was still worth living. Hope and laughter are filled with purpose. So is friendship.

You can affect people's lives by showing up, being available, and reminding them it will be okay. The gift of laughter, a few words of encouragement, a gesture of kindness. Through each of these you can add more purpose to your life. All it takes is a moment.

A Walk across the Diamond

In Brooklyn, New York, is MCU Park, home of the minor league baseball team the Brooklyn Cyclones. At the entrance of the park stands a bronze statue depicting two baseball players, one with his arm around the shoulders of the other. It represents what some have called "one of baseball's most glorious and honorable moments," a moment between Jackie Robinson and Pee Wee Reese standing together against the ugliness of racism. The statue reminds us of the power a moment of purpose can have.[3]

Jackie Robinson was the first black player to play professional baseball in the major leagues. He's a Hall of Famer and one of the best players in the game's history. April 15, 1947, was the historic day when Jackie took the field as the first baseman for the Brooklyn Dodgers. In doing so, he opened the door of integration in baseball and soon after, many other black men would play in the Major League.[4] But Jackie's storied career was anything but easy.

It was a time of deep racial tension in America, and many people in the South did not want to see baseball integrated. Most baseball team owners opposed allowing blacks to play baseball, preferring to keep America's pastime for whites only. But a baseball executive named Branch Rickey disagreed. He believed integration was inevitable, and he set out to find the right person to make history. Rickey signed Jackie Robinson to play for the Dodgers, knowing he was changing baseball forever. He also knew that Jackie would face resentment and racism from fans and players alike. But Branch Rickey thought some things were worth doing regardless of how difficult they were to do.

Jackie broke the color barrier when he took the field as the Dodgers first baseman, but baseball and its fans didn't welcome him with open arms. Spectators jeered and taunted him with racial slurs and made it clear they didn't want Jackie in a Dodgers uniform or on the baseball field. Most didn't want any black man in any baseball uniform.

Robinson also met resistance in the locker room. Players, worried about their own careers, wanted to avoid the controversy that came with the racial integration embodied by Robinson. And some players didn't want Robinson on the team at all because they were racists themselves and believed integration would ruin baseball.

Jackie loved the game, and he excelled at it, but playing baseball in the major leagues was about far more than the game. Jackie's involvement was an important moment in history. It was a significant step toward breaking down the racial divide, and it was a step forward for civil rights. But that didn't make the experience any less lonely or painful. One of the most painful experiences happened on the baseball field in Cincinnati, Ohio.

To say the fans in Cincinnati were inhospitable would be an understatement. From the moment Jackie took the field, they hurled vicious and personal insults at him. Fans in other cities had jeered and taunted, but the depth of the racial slurs and the extreme level of vitriol leveled at Jackie in Cincinnati was worse than anything he'd experienced before. One teammate, Pee Wee Reese, did something about it. Reese grew up in the South, in nearby Kentucky, where the prevailing sentiment was that blacks were inferior to whites. But standing on the field in Cincinnati that day, Reese knew that Robinson needed support.

Reese walked across the infield of the baseball diamond from his position at shortstop to where Jackie was standing near first base. Pee Wee walked up next to Jackie and put his arm around him and had a brief conversation with him.[5] The moment was palpable, and the crowd grew quiet. The jeering stopped. It was a powerful statement for Pee Wee to stand and support his black teammate. It affected the crowd watching. Pee Wee's actions spoke volumes. If a Southern Hall of Fame white player could accept a black man on the field, maybe everyone else could too.

When asked about the moment years later, Reese explained, "I was just trying to make the world a little bit better. That's what you're supposed to do with your life, isn't it?"[6] At the end of your life, wouldn't it be a wonderful thing to know that you made the world a little better? As Pee Wee said, that's what we're supposed to do with our lives. And that's what Pee Wee did for Jackie Robinson with one purposeful moment.

In a moment, Pee Wee Reese supported a teammate, silenced a racist crowd, and inspired people so much that they erected a statue memorializing the event. We can all have powerful moments of purpose by standing with someone in support. It may require you to walk a little, or stand up to the crowd. But in a moment, you can make the world a little better.

The Off-Key Guardian Angel

Natalie Gilbert aspired to be a Broadway star. When she was thirteen years old, she entered a Toyota promotional contest called Get the Feeling of a Star and she won. Her prize? She would sing the National Anthem at a Portland Trail Blazers NBA playoff game in front of 20,000 fans in the arena, and millions more on television. Natalie would soon get to experience the feeling of being a star.

On game day, Natalie woke up with the flu. She didn't want to miss her opportunity, so she arrived at the Rose Garden arena, hair up, dressed in a black and white ball gown. The energy in the arena was electric. The Trail Blazers home crowd was ready to help their team bounce back from their two-game deficit.

It began the same way every sporting event begins, with the singing of the National Anthem. The crowd stands, the announcer introduces Natalie; she takes a step forward holding a microphone; the fans cheer. A few seconds pass as Natalie prepares to sing; a hush falls over the crowd. She raises the microphone and begins, "Oh, say can you see . . ." All is going as expected until twenty seconds in when Natalie falters. She forgets the words and freezes. Ten agonizing seconds of silence follow. Natalie laughs nervously at first, then panic sets in. She looks around at the crowd in desperation. The crowd cheers to spur her on, but it does no good. She stands frozen in fear.

Then from her right, a man walks up next to Natalie, saying, "It's all right. Come on. Come on." He puts one arm around her shoulder, and with the other he raises the microphone for Natalie. He prompts her with the next words, "star light's last gleaming." Natalie gets two words out and freezes again. The man reaches for her hand and raises the microphone again so Natalie can continue, feeding her the next words to get her back on track. She makes it fifteen seconds, then falters again. He stays with her, encouraging her, singing all the while.

It's clear singing is not his thing. But this wasn't about him, it was about a thirteen-year-old, eighth-grade girl dying of embarrassment in front of 20,000 people. They press on through the anthem. He encourages the crowd to join in. With one arm still around Natalie, and the other conducting the tempo for the crowd, he and Natalie and everyone in the arena reach the glorious last few words, "and the home of the brave." The man hugs Natalie and she says, "Thank you," as relief washes over her face while the crowd cheers.[7]

Who was the man that rescued Natalie Gilbert in her moment of need? Maurice Cheeks, coach of the Portland Trail Blazers, the team in the playoffs, down two games to none. He had a lot on his mind, like winning a playoff game. Of the 20,000 people there that night, Maurice is the one who stepped up.

He would later say, "I just looked, and I knew she was struggling. I am a father. Everyone can understand that. Once I saw it, I did not want her to be standing in the middle of all those people and not know the words. So I just kind of reacted."[8]

When reporters asked Natalie about the experience, she responded, "I was turning around looking for anybody to help me. No one did anything."[9] Then Maurice Cheeks walked across the court and stood beside her. "It was like a guardian angel had come and put his arm around my shoulder and helped me get through one of the most difficult experiences I've ever had." I'm sure it's a moment Natalie will never forget, nor the millions of fans who witnessed her unintended duet with a compassionate basketball coach.

Maurice Cheeks stepped into Natalie Gilbert's moment of need. Cheeks is a Hall of Fame basketball player, an NBA coach. He is on the all-time list for career assists, but his most memorable moment on a basketball court had nothing to do with basketball, and everything to do with helping a struggling teenager.

At the end of my life, I want to have moments like the one shared between Maurice and Natalie. We all do. Be someone who steps up when no one else does. Be okay with singing out of tune if that's what it takes to help someone through their moment of need. Purpose can be found by helping people through their difficult moments.

A Bus Driver in Paris

It was a sunny October day in Paris, and Francois Le Berre was waiting to catch a bus. Francois has multiple sclerosis and is confined to a wheelchair. The bus arrived and the departing passengers filed out as the new passengers squeezed in. By the time the crowd of people had cleared, there was no room on the bus for Francois.

Every bus in Paris has designated spots to accommodate wheelchair passengers. However, on that sunny day in Paris people were crowded into those designated spaces, and no one seemed inclined to make room for Le Berre and his wheelchair.

With Le Berre still waiting on the sidewalk, the bus driver noticed that none of the passengers were making space for him to get on the bus. The driver didn't like what he was seeing. He yelled for all the passengers to get off the bus and told them they would have to wait for the next one. Then he spoke to Francois and invited him to get on the bus with his companion. Once situated, the bus departed with Le Berre and his companion on board and a crowd of people back on the sidewalk waiting for the next bus to arrive.[10]

The disabled are society's invisible people. We go about our business failing to accommodate those who need more time or help to get from place to place. The bus driver didn't turn a blind eye to Le Berre. He paid attention to him when others didn't, prioritized him, and took action to help. It was a single moment, but one filled with meaning and purpose. The driver's actions let Le Berre know that he wasn't invisible, that he was important and deserved respect like everyone else.

People who need help and advocacy are all around us. In a single moment you can find purpose by showing respect to those who are often ignored, loving those who are unloved. You can see the invisible people in the shadows of life and listen to those who are so often ignored. We can find purpose one moment at a time. It may require you to leave some people behind, but imagine the impact you can have if you help those who need it most.

Comfortable Being Uncomfortable

Nick Palermo is a dear friend I've known for decades. He had his own encounter with someone in a wheelchair, and Nick's moment of purpose changed his life forever. It began with a simple hello.

It was the fall of 1980 and Nick worked for Young Life, an

organization that works with high school students. Nick was visiting Blackford High School in San Jose when he noticed twenty-five kids in wheelchairs hanging out together at the end of the hallway. He had visited many high school campuses but had never seen so many kids in wheelchairs. Being the friendly person he is, Nick introduced himself. In his book, *Missing Stars, Fallen Sparrows*, Nick shares what happened next.

> It all started with Steve. After hearing someone calling out his name, I quickly and innocently said, 'Hi, Steve,' and put my hand out to shake his. He said something, but his speech was so garbled I couldn't understand a word. Then he reached out his hand to shake mine, and I shuttered. His hand was gnarled, like the bark of an old oak tree. I was shocked and didn't know what to do. I quickly withdrew my hand and said, 'Nice meeting you.' As another kid with slurred speech said something to me I panicked, 'Oh God,' I thought, 'what is he saying? And what am I doing here?' Then a girl in a wheelchair next to me dropped her pencil on the floor. I instinctively went to pick it up, and she drooled on my arm. That did it! Frozen by embarrassment and way beyond anything resembling my comfort zone, I quickly left.[11]

What started as a moment of kindness and purpose became minutes filled with discomfort. But over the following days, Nick thought about those kids in wheelchairs. When he returned to Blackford, he found them all together, in the same spot as before. No other students were interacting with them. A thousand teenagers paid no attention to dozens of kids in wheelchairs. It was like they were invisible. Nick felt that every one of those kids deserved moments of kindness and friendship and the gift of being seen and heard. He went back and said hello. And again, he felt out of place and uncomfortable. But he persisted. Each time Nick was on campus, he went back and talked with the kids that everyone else ignored. Nick decided he would continue going back until he got comfortable being uncomfortable.

So began Nick's four-decade adventure working with his friends with disabilities. His moment of kindness grew into a lifetime of purpose. The more time Nick spent with kids who had disabilities, the more he realized how invisible and separate they were from everybody else.

Many had never been to a movie or the mall. They'd never been to a sleepover or Disneyland. Theirs was a predictable routine with limited options. They were at home, school, or the doctor's office or being transported in a wheelchair-equipped van to one of those places. Nick decided he wanted to give them the same opportunities that able-bodied teenagers had. With no background or training working with kids with disabilities, Nick founded an organization called the Capernaum Project, and later Emmaus Inn Ministries, so he could minister to the needs of those society so often leaves behind.

What started with one group of kids with disabilities at one high school grew. Nick brought kids on ropes courses, horseback riding, and to Disneyland. He brought them to camp and held dances, which is quite a sight to watch a hundred kids cruising the dance floor in wheelchairs. Along the way, Nick told them about God and shared stories from the Bible. More than anything, he reminded them they mattered.

Over the next forty years, Capernaum grew to over two hundred ministries in twenty-eight countries. Nick has journeyed with thousands of friends with disabilities, and he's trained hundreds more to do the hard work of entering a world of discomfort and awkwardness. He passed the torch of Capernaum to others, and it continues today. Nick now works for Emmaus Inn Ministries, a nonprofit organization he founded to focus on equipping and encouraging those who work with people who have disabilities.

Nick has experienced more uncomfortable moments than anyone I know. And he has changed the lives of thousands because of it. What began as a moment of kindness became a life of purpose and has since grown into a wonderful legacy. We all want the world to be better because of something we've contributed. The world is better for thousands of people with disabilities because of all that Nick has done.

Moments of purpose may await you in uncomfortable places with uncomfortable people. The most significant impact you have with your life may start as a moment of purpose and grow into a legacy. What's outside your comfort zone? If you want to add more purpose to your life, get comfortable being uncomfortable. The world will be better because you were here.

Dancing for Mary

Sports have always been a substantial part of my life. As a kid, I played soccer and baseball. I was on the swim team, and later I was a diver. In high school I wrestled when I was small and switched to basketball once I grew. My friends and I were always doing something active—football, Wiffle Ball, ultimate Frisbee, and cliff jumping. But there was one activity I did longer than any other, one I never even acknowledged as something I did.

My parents wanted me and my sister to stay connected with our Irish heritage. When I was five, my mother put me in Irish dancing. I was not happy. I wanted nothing to do with dancing and I hoped it was a secret my friends would know nothing about.

Irish dancing is a cross between tap dancing and ballet. It embarrassed me to even be in the class, so the teacher had to give me private lessons in a storage closet of the old schoolhouse where classes took place. I would have never believed that Irish dancing would be a meaningful part of my life for almost two decades.

Three things happened that changed my perspective about dancing. First, there were a lot of cute girls. Second, I discovered I could win trophies and medals. And third, I realized I could travel to competitions across the country and to Ireland for the World Championships.

I grew to love Irish dancing and all the experiences it afforded me. It was a fantastic adventure, but still nothing I would admit to my friends. Growing up is hard enough, so I didn't think it was prudent to offer my friends information that would come back and haunt me through relentless teasing. So I kept two very separate lives, my dancing life and my regular life. The plan was to keep the two worlds apart and never have one mix with the other. The plan didn't work.

At first, keeping dancing a secret wasn't difficult. No one

asked too many questions about life in elementary school. But by the time I was in high school, it became challenging. My friends wanted to know why I was out of town so much, and they wanted to know where I was going. Several times I ended up dancing on television. The last thing I wanted was for my friends to be flipping channels on the TV and stumble across me dancing in a kilt. I did everything I could to arrange football games or lengthy bike rides on days the shows aired, making sure my friends would not be sitting in front of a television.

In my last couple of years of high school, I ran out of excuses and my two worlds collided. I was dancing at an event for St. Patrick's Day, and as I was leaving the stage, I ran into the father of one of my close friends. If I was lucky, he would drink enough that night so he wouldn't remember.

By this point I was traveling often. My friends and I were hanging out all the time, day and night, so it was obvious when I would disappear for days without explanation. By the time I reached college, a handful of my closest friends knew about my dancing.

Dan was one of those friends. I got a call from him one night and he told me his mother, Mary, was dying. Doctors said she didn't have long to live, and Dan had a favor to ask me. He told me that his mom wanted to see Irish dancing before she died, some strange remaining item on her bucket list. Dan knew I danced and asked me if I would come dance for his mother. Every fiber of my being resisted the idea. I had kept my two lives separate. The thought of dancing in front of people I knew from my regular life was more than a little uncomfortable. But every ounce of decency told me to stop thinking about myself. Someone's dying wish was more important than my discomfort.

I went to Mary's house, and we wheeled her out to the driveway, which would serve as the stage. I wore my kilt, turned on the music, and danced for Mary. And Dan, his wife, and neighbors. As luck would have it, Mary lived on a busy street, so people driving by stopped to watch. Having kept my dancing a secret for almost twenty years, it was a strange experience dancing in the street for anyone to watch. I pressed on, finished dancing, and then spent some time with Mary. She was smiling and happy and very appreciative. I was glad I could bring her joy in her last days and relieved it was over.

But it wasn't over. Mary died just a few days later. When Dan called to tell me the news, he expressed how much it meant to his mother that I had danced for her. And then he made another request. Dan's father wanted to know if I would dance at her funeral. Mary had been so thrilled to see me dance. He thought it would be a perfect way to celebrate her life and the happiness she had in her last days. I didn't want to dance for a few people gathered on the street. I really didn't want to dance in front of hundreds of people at a funeral, many I knew. But there was only one right answer to such a request. A few days later I danced at Mary's funeral, for Mary. It was the last time I ever danced.

Some moments are bigger than we are. Some of the most meaningful moments we can create are those that no one else can. A moment in time. These are moments of purpose. If you don't act, you lose the moment forever.

As you go about your days, look for the moments of purpose that only you can provide. It may require you to be vulnerable, but those might be moments that have the greatest impact. I'm glad I ignored my discomfort and seized a moment of purpose with Mary. To grant a dying wish is an extraordinary gift to add to your story. Live your life in such a way that moments of purpose fill it. Your story will be richer for it.

18

GIVE WINGS TO OTHERS

A s we continue to look for new ways to understand purpose and how to live our best lives, realize that finding your purpose may not be about you. Your greatest purpose in life may be to give wings to someone else as they try to find their purpose. Such was the case with Michael Brown.

Wings to Mockingbird

Michael was a cabaret performer and songwriter. He found his niche writing industrial musicals. These were Broadway-style musical productions that US corporations would put on for employees at events such as sales conferences or manager meetings to motivate employees or salespeople. In 1956, Brown had an excellent year, after having enormous success writing the music for a musical fashion show for *Esquire* magazine.

As the year wrapped up, Michael and his wife, Joy, hosted

a Christmas party and invited over friends and family. One of their guests was a woman named Nellie who had recently moved to Manhattan from Alabama. Nellie was an aspiring writer who came to New York to be closer to the publishing world. She found the city so expensive she had to have two jobs to make ends meet. Nellie was so busy working as an airlines reservations clerk for British Airways and a clerk at a bookstore she didn't have much time left to write. Living in the middle of the publishing universe wasn't doing her any good.

Gifts were being exchanged at the party, and Michael Brown told Nellie there was a gift for her on the tree. Hanging from the branches like an ornament, Nellie found an envelope addressed to her. She opened it and found a note inside that read, "You have one year off from your job to write whatever you please. Merry Christmas."[1]

It astounded Nellie to receive such a gift, and she tried to return it. She told Michael and Joy it was too generous and too much of a risk, but they insisted she take it. Nellie quit her two jobs and started writing, wanting to honor the Browns' gracious gift.

Nellie toiled away and wrote a novel about life as she knew it in the South. She finished the book and found a publisher willing to publish five thousand copies. Nellie published the novel using her middle name, so the world came to know her as Harper Lee. Her book? *To Kill a Mockingbird.*

Mockingbird won the Pulitzer Prize in fiction and has sold over forty million copies since its release. Published in forty languages, it still sells over 750,000 copies every year, sixty years after being published.[2] And the Browns' gift to Harper Lee made it all possible.

When Michael Brown died on June 11, 2014, the *New York Times* reported this headline: "Michael Brown, 93, Dies; Industrial Musicals Gave Wings to 'Mockingbird.'"[3] Over sixty years after placing an envelope on a tree for Nellie, the world remembered Michael for giving wings to someone else's dream. Not only did his generous gift help Harper Lee realize her purpose, but millions of people over the last six decades have gotten to experience the joy of reading her incredible book, *To Kill a Mockingbird*.

Your life may have many purposes, but don't miss the ones that may have little to do with you. You can give wings to someone else trying to find their purpose. You can play a part in someone else's journey. Your life's story includes every interaction and every contribution you make to someone else's life. Whose dreams can you give wings to? Maybe the headline in the papers about your life will tell the story of the role you played giving wings to someone else who achieved something amazing. Sounds like a wonderful headline to me.

The Jazz Singer and the Movie Star

Ella Fitzgerald is one of the most popular and accomplished jazz singers of all time. She won thirteen Grammy awards and sold over forty million records. Ella received the Recording Academy's Lifetime Achievement Award, the Society of Singers Lifetime Achievement Award, and the NAACP Lifetime Achievement Award, just to name a few of her accolades.[4] But just as Harper Lee had someone give wings to her dreams, so did Ella Fitzgerald.

Ella had a rough childhood. When she was fifteen years old, her mother died. Her stepfather was abusive, and she ended up living with an aunt in Harlem. She quit school to earn money but ended up being placed in a reform school because of her truancy. Despite the hardships, Fitzgerald soon made a name for herself in small jazz clubs across the country, impressing audiences with her amazing voice.

Despite her enormous talent, it was the 1950s, a time when black performers could not stay at many hotels and could only eat at certain restaurants. This racism extended into the performance halls and venues, so black performers found themselves relegated to the smaller jazz clubs.

Fitzgerald dreamed of playing the large, fancy clubs where the biggest stars performed, but she found those doors closed and opportunities unavailable. Ella, however, had an enormous fan in the biggest star of the day, Marilyn Monroe. The two met and became friends, and Marilyn played a key part in giving wings to Ella's dreams.

Marilyn spent hours listening to Ella Fitzgerald's records. When asked in an interview who her favorite performer was, Monroe answered, "My very favorite person, and I love her as a person as well as a singer, I think she's the greatest, and that's Ella Fitzgerald."[5] As the two became friends, Marilyn learned of the closed doors Ella encountered, and she decided she would help.

Monroe knew the owner of one of the biggest clubs in Los Angeles, the Mocambo on the Sunset Strip. Stars like Frank Sinatra played on the Mocambo stage. Even the audience was a who's who of celebrity.

Marilyn called the Mocambo owner, Charlie Morrison, and lobbied him to have Ella play the club. Morrison was reluctant. Marilyn promised that if he booked Ella to play, she would attend Ella's performances and bring her friends. Morrison was smart enough to realize the incredible publicity he would generate with Marilyn in the audience, so he agreed to book Ella Fitzgerald to perform at the Mocambo for two weeks.

True to her word, Marilyn was there, at the front of the club, for every one of Ella's performances. Frank Sinatra and Judy Garland attended Ella's first night. The evening was a monumental success, and soon every one of Ella's shows at the Mocambo sold out. Morrison added additional weeks to the contract, and Ella never looked back.

The shows at the Mocambo forever changed the trajectory of Ella Fitzgerald's career. She could now get shows at all the big and fancy clubs. And Fitzgerald recognized the role Marilyn Monroe played in her success. She said, "I owe Marilyn Monroe a real debt . . . she personally called the owner of the Mocambo, and told him she wanted me booked immediately, and if he would do it, she would take a front table every night. She told him, and it was true, due to Marilyn's superstar status, that the press would go wild. The owner said yes, and Marilyn was there, front table, every night. The press went overboard. After that, I never had to play a small jazz club again."[6]

The doors of the big clubs opened to Ella, but they weren't always the front doors. Fitzgerald still encountered racism, even as a popular star. Some venues she played insisted that Ella enter and exit through the side door of the venue because she was black.

Ella had a show in Colorado and Marilyn joined her. When they arrived at the venue, the doorman directed Fitzgerald to enter through the side entrance. This appalled Marilyn, and she refused to go inside unless she could walk through the front door with Ella. The owner relented and had Ella and Marilyn escorted into the club through the front doors. This was another turning point for Ella. Soon she was being treated with respect, welcomed through the front door of every venue she played.[7]

Marilyn Monroe and Ella Fitzgerald remained friends until Marilyn's death nine years later. But the impact of their friendship changed Ella Fitzgerald's career and life forever. Monroe stood up for Ella when she needed an advocate and helped improve her life. She used her relationship with Charlie Morrison to advocate for Fitzgerald to play the Mocambo. Marilyn agreed to attend Ella's shows and insisted that club owners treat Ella with the respect she deserved. All small actions, but each sent the same message, *I am here for you. I will help you. I am on your side.*

Marilyn's actions gave wings to Ella's dreams. We can do the same for others by standing up for them and opening doors that can help them accomplish the goals they want to achieve. Small, simple actions can change the trajectory of someone's career and their life.

Olympic Fever

When I was nineteen, a few of my friends and I did a cycling trip to Yosemite. A dozen friends were driving up to go camping, and four of us rode our bicycles the two hundred miles through the Sierra Nevada mountains. After twenty-four hours of pedaling, we rolled into the campsite and joined our friends. We camped for a week and went cliff jumping at a local swimming hole every day.

When it came time to leave, it was difficult to watch our friends pile into their cars and drive away. They would be home in five hours. We had a long day and two hundred miles of pedaling over mountains ahead of us.

The ride felt a lot harder on the way home than it had on the way to Yosemite. On the way up, there was the payoff of reaching our destination, seeing friends, and enjoying the beautiful Yosemite Valley. On the way home, it was just work. Riding through the Central Valley, the temperatures were over 100 degrees. About one hundred miles into the trip, I started feeling a sharp pain in my knee every time I pushed down on the pedal. To ease the pain, I ended up cycling fifty miles with one leg. The miles dragged on, and we realized we would not make it home that night as planned.

We rode all day and into the night and found ourselves in the most grueling part of the journey, climbing our way up hills that lasted twenty and thirty miles each. We rode in silence and darkness, having no light except for the headlights of the few cars that would pass and the dull glow of the moon. There was a small park on the far side of Livermore, which would be the first civilization we would see after spending hours riding through the unpopulated mountains. We decided we would stop at the park to sleep for the night and finish our journey the next day.

We were struggling to keep pedaling by the time we saw the lights of Livermore. None of us had any energy left. All we could think about was getting to the park and sleeping. Then the strangest thing happened. As we turned the corner from the unlit mountain road, we were shocked to see the tiny town of Livermore bustling with cars and people. The streets were at a near standstill, and people packed the sidewalks from curb to storefront. We couldn't understand how the sleepy town of Livermore was brimming with life at 11:00 p.m.

Then we saw the signs. It was National Cruising Night, and people had gathered from far and wide to watch the custom lowriders cruising down the street. It was a warm summer night, and it was just a few days before the Olympics were being held in Los Angeles. Olympic fever was in the air.

As soon as we turned onto the crowded street, the people packed onto the sidewalks started cheering for us, a scraggly bunch of bone-weary, exhausted nineteen-year-olds. Their energy was infectious. The more they cheered, the faster we pedaled. Soon the crowds were chanting "USA, USA, USA" as we passed through the town. It was illogical. It was obvious we had nothing to do with the Olympics. We weren't wearing red, white, or blue. We didn't have any American flags. But something struck a chord in the crowd to see four ragged cyclists come out of the mountains late at night with packs and sleeping bags and pots strapped to our bicycles.

By the time we reached the far end of town, we were pedaling hard and moving fast. The adrenaline was pumping, and the crowd cheered us on the entire way. When we reached the park, we looked at each other and couldn't imagine stopping. We had bounds of energy, spurred to life by the enthusiastic crowd. We were ready to push through the last mountain pass for the final thirty-five miles.

I'm certain we wouldn't have made it home that night without the cheers and encouragement of the frenzied crowd.

It wasn't life or death, or even important, but it showed me what it feels like to have someone give wings to what you are doing. That crowd gave us energy where there was none, and they helped us achieve what we would have thought impossible.

You need not know someone to give wings to their endeavors. You can encourage and cheer on anyone. When you support people and give wings to their dreams, you bring energy and hope and possibility. You help people overcome obstacles and achieve the impossible.

Keep your eyes open. You never know where you will find someone in need of wings. I wasn't expecting to experience what we did in Livermore, the sleepy town at the base of the mountains. It was a wonderful reminder of the power of encouragement. Who can you encourage by giving wings to their dreams?

A Long Way from London

Edward was a shy kid. Making matters worse, an operation gone awry left him with a lazy eye and a stutter. Add to that the thick glasses he wore to correct his eyesight and his spiky red hair, and he was a sure target for the bullies at his school.

His stutter made him self-conscious. When he tried to answer questions in class he often froze, speechless, afraid he would stutter when speaking in front of everyone. This only made him withdraw and not take part, hoping it would spare him the embarrassment. He went to speech therapy for help, but he wasn't seeing much progress. Then he discovered Eminem.

Edward had found sanctuary in music as a kid. He sang in

the church choir since the age of four and enjoyed playing the guitar in his room. When his father brought him an album by Eminem, the speed of the lyrics astonished Edward. He listened to the album over and over, learning every word along the way. Then he made a surprising discovery. When he was singing along with the album, his stutter disappeared. This encouraged Edward to dive deeper into music. He began writing his own songs and continued to improve his guitar skills. By the time he was fourteen, he was ready to hit the road.[8]

With a few things packed and his guitar in hand, Edward set out for London. He was ready to bring his music to the world. He played on the streets and looked for opportunities to play anywhere he could. Edward auditioned, collaborated, recorded, and played his songs for anyone who would listen. He slept on couches, in parks, anywhere he could find. By the time he was eighteen, he was playing three hundred shows a year. It was time for another big move.

At nineteen, Edward moved to America to pursue a career in music. He arrived with nothing. No recording contract, no shows, and no place to stay. He repeated what he'd done in London, playing on the streets and looking for any opportunity to perform. He sent his music to anyone he could find related to the music business, but he wasn't getting much of a response. In fact, he heard from only one person, the host of a local radio show. They invited him to perform on the show.

The radio show was *The Jamie Fox Show*, hosted by film star and singer Jamie Foxx. Edward played live on the air, and Jamie thought he was incredible. When he found out Edward had nowhere to stay, Jamie invited him to his house. With that invitation, Edward slept on Foxx's couch for the next six weeks. He used the recording studio at Jamie's house to record more of his music. And then Jamie opened one more door for Edward. He brought him to an open mic event in Los Angeles, walked him to the stage, and introduced Ed Sheeran to the crowd.

When the redheaded white guy walked out on the stage holding a ukulele, the predominantly black crowd of eight hundred people was in disbelief. Then Ed sang. He finished twelve minutes later to a standing ovation. He had won the crowd over.[9]

Doors continued to open for the talented redhead from England. He released his first studio album in 2011, which was an enormous hit, selling over four million copies. His first four albums have all hit number one on the charts, he won a Grammy for Song of the Year, and his songs have over one billion views on YouTube.[10]

Ed Sheeran is very talented, but he still needed help along the way. When he had no shows, no recording contract, and no place to stay, Jamie Foxx gave wings to Ed's dreams. Jamie said yes when others said no or didn't reply at all. He shared what he had with Ed. He gave him a place to sleep and food to eat, and he let him use his recording studio. Jamie took a risk and opened doors for Ed. He endorsed Sheeran and gave him a chance to take the stage in front of eight hundred of his peers, knowing a redhead from London was not what the audience was expecting. Giving wings to someone else's dreams gives you a chance to share in their story, just as Jamie got to share a part in Ed's.

Aesop, famous for his fables, noted, "No act of kindness, no matter how small, is ever wasted." We can play a meaningful part in people's lives with simple acts of kindness.

Jamie shared his home, shared the stage, and gave Ed an opportunity. But before all of that, Jamie responded when no one else did. That put everything else in motion. Do you have some unanswered requests waiting for you? Maybe you can give wings to somebody's dreams by responding and sharing what you've got with them.

Starry Night

What if everybody found someone like Jamie Foxx or Marilyn Monroe or Michael Brown to give wings to their dreams? Someone who believed in them, supported them, advocated for them, cheered them on. How many more people would flourish and succeed? So many toil away in anonymity, never receiving encouragement, help, or recognition. No person's life shows this more than the tragic life of Vincent van Gogh.

Van Gogh is one of the most influential artists in history. If you look at the highest-priced paintings ever sold at auction, van Gogh is one of the most represented artists on the list. This doesn't include most of his best-known works because they've never sold at auction before. His best-known paintings are hanging in the world's finest museums. When asked to place a value on van Gogh's masterpieces, museums have said they couldn't because they are priceless. Evan Beard believed you could.

Beard is the National Art Services Executive at Bank of America Private Bank. He's an expert in the art world. He wanted to put a price tag on the greatest paintings hanging in museums, so he spoke with several of the world's top art collectors and dealers and asked them what paintings they would want to buy and how much they would pay. Second only to a painting by Picasso was van Gogh's *Starry Night*. The estimated price tag? $1 billion.[11]

What makes this more remarkable is that van Gogh sold only one painting during his lifetime, *The Red Vineyard*, for only 400 francs (about $2,000 today). Over his ten-year painting career, he produced almost 900 paintings and 1,100 sketches and drawings.[12] Despite his prolific output, van Gogh's work was all but ignored.

At thirty-seven years old, Vincent van Gogh gave up. He shot himself in the abdomen with a revolver in a field close to the boarding house where he lived in the French countryside of Auvers. He died believing he was a failure and that no one had any interest in the art he had poured himself into.

What if someone had given wings to van Gogh's dreams? What masterpieces would he have produced if he'd lived another thirty or forty years? It's tragic to realize that someone whose work is so renowned and admired today died never knowing how deeply people would come to appreciate his work. I don't think van Gogh is alone.

There is unrecognized genius all around us. People who have the talent to create masterpieces but are missing someone to give wings to their dreams. Are you taking the time to notice the genius of those around you?

Kind words can last a lifetime. Your words can encourage the unrecognized people who are losing hope. Your encouragement can remind people what they do matters, that they matter. You can be someone who gives wings to others through kind words and encouragement. Recognize the talented people around you. Encourage them. You may give wings to the next van Gogh.

19

PERSONAL PURPOSE

If you want to find more purpose in your life, get personal. The shaping events in your life and the causes that stir you most are fertile ground for adding purpose to your life. Personal purpose brings together your desire to make a difference in the world and the causes that mean the most to you. This is a powerful combination with the potential to affect people. It's not just doing something good, it's doing something good because of what it means to you.

Still Giving Thanks

Tony Robbins is a bestselling author and speaker, and he's well known for his personal development events. Two of his bestselling books, *Awaken the Giant Within* and *Unlimited Power*, capture the essence of his work, helping people put the practices in place to achieve outstanding success. But beyond his work, Robbins has found purpose in hunger relief, something that's deeply personal to him.

For years, Robbins has provided meals to families on Thanksgiving Day. He has now partnered with a charity organization called Feeding America with the goal of providing one billion meals to hungry families by 2025. When asked about his involvement, Tony states the statistics. Almost fifty million people in the United States go to sleep not sure if they will have enough to eat the next day. Then he adds his story, "I know that those are more than startling statistics—those numbers are human beings suffering—and I came from one of those families."[1] Why did he get involved? Because he knows what it's like to worry about food. It's personal.

Tony had a tough family life growing up. His parents divorced when he was seven years old, his mom remarried a few times, money was always tight, and his home life was chaotic and abusive. On Thanksgiving Day, when Tony was eleven, he knew there wouldn't be any Thanksgiving Day feast. His parents were arguing and there was no food in the house. Then someone knocked on their front door. It was a man holding bags of groceries, his gift to the Robbins' family.[2] Tony says, "I'll never forget what it felt like as a young boy thinking we wouldn't be able to sit down to Thanksgiving dinner. Then a stranger gave us the food we couldn't afford."[3]

Tony decided he wanted to give others the same gift he received as a kid, the gift of a meal to someone without food. He remembered what it felt like to hear an unexpected knock at the door. Tony remembered the feeling of being confused, then shocked, to realize that a stranger cared enough about him and his family to give them food so they could enjoy Thanksgiving.

When you've been in a situation and lived it, you can

understand and empathize with those there now. You know how much it means to get help. You can help bring about better outcomes. Our experiences equip us to assist others going through what we went through. Draw from the shaping experiences of your life, and you will add purpose to yours.

The Gift of Freedom

Few things boggle my mind more than the practice of slavery. To imagine any person being owned by another is incomprehensible. Slave owners in America deprived slaves of their freedom, tore apart families, and subjected them to violence and rape. Can you imagine being a slave? Not for a day or a year, but for a lifetime, knowing your life was not your own.

Escape would be the only relief from the unbearable existence of plantation life. But the penalties for attempting escape were severe, so much so that most slaves never risked it. But one woman saw no other option for her life. Her name was Harriet Tubman.

Harriet was born a slave in Maryland and lived the grinding existence of a plantation slave. Her owner whipped and beat her so severely she carried the scars and damage the rest of her life. When she was twelve, she suffered a life-altering injury at the hands of a neighboring slave owner. Harriet was picking up groceries from the store when the plantation owner saw one of his slaves trying to escape. Rather than help restrain the escaping slave, Harriet helped him escape by blocking the doorway so the slave owner couldn't give chase. The slave owner was furious and heaved a two-pound metal weight at Harriet's head. The weight knocked her out, and she remained unconscious for two days. It took months for her to recover, and the injury left Tubman with seizures and severe headaches for the rest of her life.[4]

After nearly three decades as a slave, Tubman was ready to risk it all to pursue her freedom. She would later say, "I had reasoned out this in my mind: there was one of two things I had a right to, liberty or death; if I could not have one, I would have the other; for no man should take me alive."[5]

On September 17, 1849, Tubman and two of her brothers ran away. A few weeks into their escape, the brothers saw posters offering a reward for their capture and return. They turned back, afraid their risk of capture was too high. Harriet led the way back to the plantation, but she had no intention of staying. A few weeks later, Tubman escaped again, this time on her own.

Harriet successfully traveled ninety miles to Pennsylvania. She was free. But Harriet was not content with her own freedom. She wanted her family and others to experience liberty. Harriet returned to her plantation in the South to help her family escape. It was risky. She knew if they caught her she would lose her freedom forever. But this was a personal pursuit for Harriet, regardless of the risk. She said, "Slavery is the next thing to hell."[6] Determined to help, she returned to lead her people out of the hell of slavery and into the promised land of freedom.

Harriet Tubman made three trips back to her plantation, each time to rescue more family members and friends. She became the conductor of the Underground Railroad, a network of people offering shelter in private homes and churches to help escaped slaves get to the North, and freedom. From the time she escaped until the end of the Civil War, Tubman returned to the South nineteen times, risking everything each time she returned. She led over three hundred slaves to freedom, never losing one along the way. After the Civil War, Tubman helped impoverished former slaves adjust to their new and still challenging lives of freedom.[7]

For Harriet Tubman, helping people escape the horrors of slavery was a purpose as personal as it could be. She knew the abhorrent conditions slaves suffered, and she knew what it meant to be free. It was something Tubman wanted for everyone. Do you have a conviction so strong you would risk it all to help others? What part of your story calls you to action? That's the place to pursue your personal purpose and add to the story of your life.

A Picture Is Worth a Thousand Convictions

Lois Gibson has been drawing portraits for over thirty years. She's very good. According to the *Guinness Book of World Records*, Lois is the best. Her drawings aren't hanging in museums, they're pinned to bulletin boards in police stations. Lois Gibson is the most successful forensic artist in history. And for Lois, it's personal.

When Gibson was a twenty-one-year-old aspiring actress, someone she thought was a neighbor knocked on her door. When she answered, a man forced his way inside and attacked her. He sexually assaulted her and choked her until she lost consciousness. Lois woke up and found her attacker gone.

She was too frightened and traumatized to do anything.

She stayed in her apartment for weeks, never reporting the incident to the police. Ultimately, Lois left Los Angeles. She moved to Texas for a fresh start and pursued a degree in fine arts at the University of Texas.

Nine years later, Lois saw a news report on television about the sexual assault of a dance teacher. The assailant raped the teacher at the dance studio in front of her students. Lois remembers, "I felt a flash of white-hot fury and a thought crossed my mind—I couldn't bear the thought of him and other criminals walking free."[8]

Gibson had an idea. She knew if she could speak to the witnesses, she could draw a picture of the assailant based on their description. This could help the police find the suspect. She recalls, "I felt compelled to use this talent to help victims of crime."[9]

Lois took action. She went to the Houston Police Department and convinced them she could help. And help she did. Over the next thirty years, Lois would draw thousands of sketches of suspects described to her by victims and witnesses. Her sketches helped achieve over 1,000 convictions. Lois's success as a sketch artist has earned her a record with Guinness World Records as the artist who has positively identified the most criminals as a forensic artist.[10]

This wasn't just work for Lois, it was more than that. She remembers being attacked and feeling helpless. She remembers how afraid she was afterward. And she realized that she could use her talents to help get the terrible people who commit those crimes off the street. Lois realized she could help bring justice and restore a sense of peace to victims. She felt compelled to help.

What compels you? Maybe you've had experiences that

give you a unique understanding or point of view. Perhaps you have a unique set of skills. Lois had success putting together her experiences and her skills to make a significant impact with her life. What impact could you have if you combined your personal experiences and your skills? The experiences related to your own life may be your most impactful pursuits. What have your life experiences prepared you to do for others? That's how you can add more purpose to your life.

The Patient Pursuit of Purpose

Uganda has one of the fastest-growing populations in the world. The country went through decades of civil war. And while the fighting ended in 2006, the Ugandan people still feel the impact of the war today.

Forced migrations were commonplace. Displaced people settled elsewhere and resettled again. When the war ended, many returned to their homes to find other people living there. Poor record-keeping, changing laws, and corruption only added to the chaos. This created the perfect environment for fraudsters to exploit an already tense situation. Land disputes are ongoing for about 50 percent of landowners in Uganda.[11]

When Jordan Kinyera was six years old, his father lost his land in a dispute. Jordan's family had been on the land for generations and had even buried relatives there. Regardless, they still lost the land.

The system can't handle the overwhelming number of cases, so disputes drag on for years. In a country of forty-one million people, there are only 3,200 lawyers. For comparison, the state of California has forty million people and over 170,000 lawyers. The shortage of lawyers in Uganda ensures that cases drag on much longer than they should.[12]

Seeing his father lose his land left a deep impression on Jordan. He saw his father become depressed and broken. Jordan remembers, "My dad was retired, so he didn't have a lot of resources. . . . He was desperate and there is something dehumanizing about being in a desperate situation and not being able to do something about it."[13] Jordan committed to getting his father's land back.

For the next eighteen years, Jordan never lost sight of his goal. He continued his education until he completed law school. Jordan said, "[I was] inspired by events I grew up witnessing, the circumstances and frustrations my family went through."[14] For Jordan, it was personal and his purpose was clear. He would use his skills as a lawyer to get his father's land back through the courts.

Jordan's first legal case was his father's land dispute. Over two decades had passed since his father had lost the family land. But Jordan's moment had arrived. He made his case before the High Court of Uganda, and the judge ruled in his father's favor. The land belonged to the Kinyera family again.

As a six-year-old, it deeply affected Jordan to witness his father lose their property. He committed the next twenty-three years of his life in patient pursuit of a single purpose, to get his father's land back. When we find a purpose to pursue that is personal to us, it creates a drive that can sustain us for decades.

Is there anything so important to you you'd be willing to pursue it for years? You can only realize some hopes and dreams if you persist long enough to succeed. Helen Keller noted, "We can do anything we want to do if we stick to it long enough." What passions and purpose can you pursue with perseverance that will make someone's world a better place years from now? Will you restore justice? Help the hungry? Right the wrongs of the past and bring the promise of a better future? Find a purpose personal to you, and pursue it for as long as it takes. Not only will you improve your life's story, but you will find success in greater measure and meaning.

For the Want of Water

When I woke up from my transplant surgery, I was in pain. Having your body cut open, unpacked, and put back together with thousands of stitches and staples is traumatic. But the toughest part of the healing process was how desperately thirsty I was after waking up.

After twelve hours in surgery my body was weak, and the doctors monitored me closely to make sure there were no complications. I couldn't eat or drink anything to minimize the chances of throwing up, which could tear out the stitches holding me together. My mouth was parched. All I could think about was how thirsty I was. I would have paid $1,000 for a glass of water. I pleaded with doctors and nurses to give me a drink. For three days the answer was always no. Those were the hardest three days of my life.

On the fourth day the doctor finally permitted me to take small sips of water. By then I was like a junkie begging for a fix, only the drug I craved was water. I can't say I've ever appreciated a glass of water as much in my life.

It's easy to take water for granted. It's everywhere. Iced

water, sparkling water, flavored water. We have bottled water and clean water from the faucet. For the few days I went without water, it was hell. When I was healthy enough to drink, I had all the water I wanted. I realized that for many, that's not the case.

About 790 million people do not have access to clean water. That's 1 in 10 people around the world. Approximately 840,000 people die each year from illness caused by drinking unsafe water. And women and children spend a staggering 200 million hours every day gathering water from far-away sources, often already contaminated.[15] I struggled for three days without water, and millions of people struggle every day. It thrilled me to find out there were organizations dedicated to solving the problem of access to clean water.

Living Water and charity: water are two organizations making an enormous impact on getting clean water to people. Both organizations dig wells in communities around the world that don't have access to clean water. The wells they've installed bring clean water to millions of people every day. It's an incredible mission, bringing the gift of water to the thirsty, improving sanitation and health conditions, and changing lives.

The purpose of these organizations strikes a chord with me. I've watched videos of the first moments a new well sprays water from the ground. I've seen how people in those communities rejoice. They won't have to walk rugged miles to retrieve and carry back heavy water jugs anymore. People can bathe and feel clean. They can quench their thirst anytime they want with clean water that is nearby and accessible. And the people will suffer less sickness. I appreciate that I can donate to organizations like charity: water and Living Water so I can share in their work bringing clean water to people who are dying of thirst.

When purpose is personal, it satisfies your soul. I love that I can help bring water to the thirsty by supporting wonderful organizations doing this meaningful work. I encourage you to find people and organizations doing work that matters to you. Get involved. Purpose that's personal can add amazing chapters to your story.

20

UNEXPECTED PURPOSE

S ometimes we pursue opportunities that interest us, but sometimes opportunities arrive unannounced at our door. While these opportunities are unexpected, they can be filled with purpose. The question is whether we will respond.

Finding more purpose sometimes has more to do with our availability than a lack of opportunity, The opportunity to find purpose surrounds us every day, but it requires us to look and notice and care enough to take action.

Angel of the Gap

In Sydney, Australia, along the rugged coastline facing the Tasman Sea, there is an ocean cliff on the South Head peninsula known as The Gap. It's a popular destination for tourists. It's also a popular destination for people who have given up hope. The Gap, known for its one-hundred-foot tall cliffs, has become a place for people wanting to end their lives.

Don Ritchie lived across the street from The Gap for

almost fifty years. He had a picturesque view of the ocean from his living room window, which also put him in a position to see the downhearted people arrive intent on ending their lives. Don couldn't just sit there and watch people step off the edge. He had to help them.

When he saw someone alone approaching the cliffs, he would walk across the street, smile, and ask, "Can I help you in some way?"[1] He would keep talking until he could convince them to step back from the cliff. When he was younger, he would restrain people while his wife called the police for help. As he got older, he would invite them back to his house for tea to talk about what was bothering them.

Authorities credit Don Ritchie with saving at least 160 people from suicide. Some estimates put the number closer to 500. Don became known as the Angel of the Gap for his lifesaving interventions.[2] Don found purpose in helping the hopeless people he saw while looking out his window.

He kept a watchful eye and took action when he noticed someone who seemed like they needed help. This turned into fifty years of purpose. He received letters, gifts, and visits from those he saved, sometimes decades later. All saying the same thing. Thank you for saving my life.[3]

Maybe your opportunity for more purpose is right outside your window. Look. Is there a lonely neighbor? What about your mail carrier or the people who deliver packages to your door? Maybe your purpose is in caring for the people who visit your home, your children's friends, colleagues you invite over for dinner. You can stand in the gap for people needing a helping hand. Your unexpected opportunity for purpose may be closer than you think.

Refugees at the Gate

Chiune Sugihara worked as a diplomat in Lithuania during WWII. He was from Japan and was sent to Lithuania in 1940 to collect intelligence on the rising unrest in Europe. When the Soviet Union invaded Poland a few months earlier, Polish exiles flooded into Lithuania. When the Soviet Union occupied Lithuania, those same refugees were desperately searching for somewhere else to flee. Sugihara found himself with an unexpected opportunity to help, but it would cost him.

Scores of refugees, many of whom were Jewish, gathered at the gates of the Japanese consulate, where Sugihara and his family lived. The refugees were hoping to get travel visas so they could escape to safety. Sugihara notified his superiors in Tokyo about the refugees and asked for instructions. Their response was explicit. Do not issue visas to anyone unless they have the needed paperwork.

Unfortunately, most of the refugees gathering at the gates had no paperwork. The scene continued to grow more dire. The crowds grew larger, as did their desperation. Chiune made another request to Tokyo, asking permission to help the refugees at his gates, and again they denied his request.

When the Soviet Union invaded Lithuania, it became clear to Sugihara that he and his family would no longer be safe at the consulate. With time and opportunity slipping away, Sugihara decided that he would defy the orders of his superiors to help the desperate refugees. He began issuing travel visas to those gathered at the gates even though they didn't have the paperwork required to receive a visa. Every visa he issued meant another family could find their way to safety. This was especially true for the Jewish families, because it was clear the Jews of Europe were in grave danger.

Over the next six weeks, Sugihara worked eighteen-hour days handwriting 2,139 transit visas to help the refugees. He also negotiated with Moscow to ensure safe passage of the Jewish refugees through the Soviet Union. Six weeks later, Tokyo ordered Sugihara and his family to leave Lithuania. It's estimated that Chiune Sugihara's visas saved over 6,000 people.[4]

His actions weren't without consequence. Having defied the orders of his superiors, the Japanese Ministry of Foreign Affairs forced Chiune to leave his job. He eventually left Japan to live in Moscow.

In 1984, Israel declared Chiune Sugihara "righteous among the nations" for saving the lives of so many Jews. The Lithuanian government designated 2020 "the year of Chiune Sugihara."[5] It's estimated that there are over 100,000 descendants of those who received a transit visa from Sugihara. When the moment presented itself, Chiune acted purposefully, and his actions saved lives.

What will you do when an unexpected opportunity with purpose presents itself? Acting may have consequences. You may have to break the rules. Sometimes purpose is costly. Are you willing to pay the price?

We would know nothing of Chiune Sugihara had he gone about his business at the consulate and obeyed the orders given to him by his superiors. Instead, he did what he thought was right and saved 6,000 people, and the tens of thousands of descendants that came after. Did he make the right choice? Absolutely! The question is, will you? When an unexpected opportunity with purpose knocks at your door, will you answer?

A Tale of Two Tricias

Tricia Seaman is an oncology nurse in Pennsylvania. She has a job rich with opportunities to help sick people in need. It's a job filled with purpose every day as she cares for her patients. But in March 2014, an unexpected opportunity to help someone changed several lives forever.

Tricia Seaman made her rounds and checked in on a new patient. The patient's name was also Tricia, Tricia Somers, and she had cancer. Seaman also read in Somers's medical chart that Somers was a single parent of an eight-year-old son and had no other family in the area.

Somers woke up from her anesthesia and was groggy. Tricia Seaman introduced herself and finished updating the medical chart. Seaman was about to leave but paused because Somers was there alone. No get-well balloons, just a few drawings from her son. Tricia sat down and asked Somers to share her story.

Tricia Somers showed Seaman pictures of her son, Wesley. His father was no longer in the picture. Tricia and her ex-husband had an abusive, violent relationship, and she left with Wesley to get a fresh start. They lived in a small apartment with their dog, Molly, a Bernese mountain dog. Tricia's parents were both gone. Cancer. The two Tricias talked for an hour. Seaman needed to see other patients, so the two said goodbye.

In the following days, Tricia Seaman was no longer Somers's attending nurse, but she visited each time she was on duty. Three weeks later, Somers was getting ready to leave the hospital. Tricia Seaman stopped by her room to say goodbye.

When she walked in the room, she saw Somers stone-faced and serious talking to someone from the hospital. Somers asked her to stay, saying, "I'm glad you stopped in because I have a question to ask you." She had received news from her doctor that she was terminal with only months to live. She looked at Tricia Seaman and asked, "When I die, will you and your husband raise my son?" An unexpected opportunity had arrived.

Tricia Seaman couldn't comprehend what she was hearing. Here was a woman she hardly knew. They had gotten to know each other a little during Somers's three weeks in the hospital, but they knew almost nothing about each other. And the request? It was life changing for everyone.

Seaman and her husband already had four kids at home. And yet she couldn't help but think about how difficult it must be for Somers to know she would not be around to take care of her son. Wesley had nowhere to go. Seaman didn't give Somers an answer but encouraged her to give her options some additional thought.

Seaman talked to her husband, Dan, about Somers's request. Neither knew the right answer, but they were certain they should stay in touch with Somers and help her through this troublesome time in her life.

The two families started spending time together. Somers was struggling to take care of Wesley and herself, so Dan and Tricia invited Somers and Wesley to come live with them. This was just two months after the two Tricias had met.

Tricia and Wesley became part of the Seaman family. They

vacationed together and grew very close. Somers continued to decline, and as the inevitable approached, they all agreed that Wesley would stay and become a part of the Seaman family. Tricia Somers died in December, at peace because she knew Dan and Tricia would take care of Wesley.

Few of us will ever receive a request as significant as the one asked of Tricia Seaman. Tricia Somers was alone in the greatest struggle of her life. She needed help, and she reached out to Tricia Seaman with an extraordinary request filled with as much purpose as any could have. The opportunity was unexpected, but Tricia and Dan embraced it.

It's an extraordinary chapter in each of their stories. Somers was brave enough to ask, and Dan and Tricia were courageous enough to say yes. There was sacrifice and change required, but the Seamans' decision to get involved made the world better for Wesley and his mom.[6]

When an unexpected opportunity knocks on your door, it will probably involve sacrifice. But if you say yes, and get involved, you can add wonderful and unexpected chapters to your story. If you want more purpose in your life, consider even the most audacious and unexpected requests. They may help you make the most of your one wild and precious life.

Everybody, Always

If I had to pick one person in the world who finds the most purpose-filled opportunities, it would be Bob Goff, hands down. He has so many amazing stories he could fill books with his adventures. In fact, he's filled two, and they're both fantastic. *Love Does* and *Everybody Always* are both *New York*

Times bestsellers, and they both showcase Bob's philosophy of living an incredible life in an ordinary world.

As Bob was trying to figure out how he wanted to live his life, he settled on one overarching principle. The best way to live life is to love everybody, always. He says, "That's our job. It's always been our job. We're supposed to just love the people in front of us."

These aren't hollow words. They serve as Bob's guiding principle for how he reacts to life's messy and unexpected circumstances. This is Bob's approach with likable people, and anyone else Bob meets along the way. And he has experienced some unique situations trying to love the people in front of him.

Bob calls himself a recovering lawyer. He is a professor and runs a nonprofit called Love Does that has been fighting for human rights and educating children in conflict zones for over fifteen years. Bob decided that to love the people in front of him he needed to act, not talk because, "Only action becomes love." I highly recommend you read his books so you can see for yourself how Bob puts love into action. But here are a few examples of how he has pursued his purpose of loving the people he encounters in everyday life.

Bob travels a lot. As a lawyer he commuted from his home in San Diego to his office in Seattle. The work he does with Love Does takes him to places like Afghanistan, Uganda, Iraq, and Somalia. He spends a lot of time in airports. Long lines and TSA check-ins are a normal part of Bob's week. One day the lines were longer than usual, and the crowds were grumpy. The unfortunate recipient of the impatient travelers was the TSA agent checking identification for every passenger. When it was Bob's turn, he did what he always did. He asked himself, *How can I love the people in front of me?* So Bob introduced himself and said, "I just wanted to thank you for the way you treat each person in line." The TSA agent paused, stepped out from behind his desk, and threw his arms around Bob. Thus began a yearslong friendship between Bob and Adrien, the TSA agent.

Each time Bob went to the airport, he would spend a few minutes learning more about Adrien. Bob rightfully noted, "Friendships can last a lifetime, but we make them three minutes at a time." The two got to know each other and talked about their families. Eventually the families met, shared meals, and spent holidays together. Bob is the only person I know who can encounter a stranger in line and become close friends. That's what it means to love the people in front of you.

Bob found another opportunity to care for a stranger when he encountered a homeless man in his car. Bob finished his last meeting of the day and went to his car to head home. There in the front seat he found a homeless man just sitting. Bob loves the people in front of him, so he seized the opportunity to respond with love. He knocked on the window and said hello. He told the homeless man he needed his car because it was time to leave. They exchanged some light-hearted banter, and the man went on his way. Bob didn't call the police or yell at him. He said hello and treated him with respect. The following day Bob went to his car and once again, sitting in the front seat was the same homeless man. They exchanged pleasantries and parted ways. And thus began an "arrangement" where a homeless man took shelter in Bob's car every day and Bob lived his beliefs that only action becomes love.

My favorite example of Bob seizing the opportunity to love the people in front of him is about Carol, a widow who moved into the house across the street from Bob. Theirs was a beautiful relationship, but I'll leave you to read the details in Bob's book *Everybody Always*.[7] Bob's approach to life has translated to countless stories of opportunities he filled with purpose. Each of these encounters adds to Bob's incredible story. What about you? Don't you want to have stories like that in your life? The unexpected. The unique. The stories people share about you at your funeral. Stories of a life filled with purpose and meaning.

I had just finished reading *Everybody Always*, and I was sitting in the cafe at work. I noticed a small woman working behind the counter. She was working hard but had a smile on her face and was noticeably pleasant to everyone crowded around to get food. All I could think of was Bob's encounters with Adrien, the TSA guy. I was curious. So when there was a lull in the line, I went over to the woman and I introduced myself. I told her I noticed how kind she was to everyone she met and I just wanted to say how wonderful that was to see. She stopped what she was doing, walked out from behind the counter, and threw her arms around me in the warmest hug. She told me her name was Lupe, and she thanked me for making her day so special.

When a stranger's kind words can move a TSA agent and a food server enough to elicit spontaneous hugs, you realize the opportunities with purpose are endless. You can find moments of opportunity every day if you will love the people in front of you. Make the most of the opportunities that come your way. You may just get an unexpected hug out of it.

Christmas in September

In May 2018, Todd and Shilo Allen heard news no parent ever wants to hear. Their beautiful two-year-old boy, Brody, had an aggressive form of brain cancer, one for which there was no treatment available. In August, the doctors told Todd and Shilo that Brody had about two months left to live.

Brody loved Christmas, and Todd and Shilo realized it was unlikely Brody would live to see another. They decided that Christmas would come in September so Brody could experience his favorite holiday one more time.

The Allens got out their Christmas decorations but wanted to make it extraordinary for Brody's last Christmas. It's difficult to find Christmas decorations in September. The Allens posted a note on Facebook asking neighbors if they could help provide more decorations. People arrived, dropping off lights and other Christmas decor.

Soon the neighbors joined in. Wanting to make Brody's last Christmas special, they all celebrated Christmas in September. They put up their own lights and hung snowflakes and garland and decorated as if it was December.[8] With the neighborhood in the holiday spirit, they took it one step further, holding a Christmas parade complete with a fire truck and Santa.

Brody loved the Christmas festivities. He loved the lights and the parade and the gifts brought to him by kind neighbors. Brody died on October 19, just a few weeks after his Christmas in September.[9] It's a Christmas no one involved will ever forget.

Sometimes purposeful opportunities will require some creative and unconventional thinking, like celebrating

Christmas in September. But if that's what it takes to support a family about to lose their child, then get out the decorations regardless of what the calendar says. That's the thing about purposeful opportunities. You don't know what they'll look like until they show up. If you want more purpose in your life, get comfortable with the unconventional and join in the festivities whenever they might be.

A Bag Full of Money

When I was thirty years old, I welcomed my first child into the world. Two days after Christmas, Aidan was born, and the adventure of parenting began. Six weeks later, I lost my job. It was a scary time. I didn't know how I would provide for my family.

I was employed with an organization called Young Life, a Christian nonprofit working with middle school and high school students. There were two distinct parts of the job, spending time with students and raising money. I loved the time with kids. It was about building relationships, doing fun and adventurous activities, and getting to tell students about God's love. We backpacked across the Rocky Mountains, went on beach trips and ski trips, built houses for the homeless in Mexico, and had summer camps guaranteed to be the best week of a kid's life.

The part I didn't enjoy was raising money. As with all nonprofit organizations, fundraising is a significant part of the job. Sometimes this meant hosting fundraising banquets or golf tournaments; often it meant meeting with individuals, explaining the work we were doing and asking if they wanted to be financially involved. While I believed deeply in the work of Young Life, asking people to donate money is difficult and humbling. Relationships are important to me, and the last thing I wanted was for anyone to feel that my time spent with them was about getting them to give money.

My first three years on Young Life staff I was part of a larger region, with several other people on staff. They were more seasoned and effective at fundraising, so my livelihood wasn't entirely dependent on my fundraising success. After three years I began developing an area that didn't have Young Life, which was exciting, but it also meant that I would need to spend more time fundraising.

The area I was developing was Saratoga, California, a very affluent community. Despite the community's wealth, raising money was a struggle from the beginning. The work we were doing with high school and middle school kids was thriving, but the lack of funding was a constant pressure. I spent three years in Saratoga and struggled financially the entire time. Aidan was born as the area slipped into deficit. There wasn't enough money to continue. Young Life put me on an unpaid leave until there was enough money to erase the deficit and meet the ongoing operating expenses for the area.

I worked without pay for a few weeks while trying to raise money, but the financial shortfall was both a short-term and long-term issue. It was over. After six years working for Young Life, I was without a job, had a new baby at home, had no money, and had no prospect for getting a job quickly. It was an anxiety-filled and unsettling time.

I didn't know what I would do next. What's the logical career move when your experience is working with middle school and high school kids for a nonprofit? The most pressing questions were all about how I would pay my bills.

Even when I was getting paid, I made little, so I had almost no savings.

I was trying my best to relish the joy of my new son, but I was deeply weighed down by the financial pressure of providing for my family. One day during my leave, there was a knock at the door. I opened it to find Dave Walsh standing on my doorstep. Dave was my Young Life leader when I was in high school. He was a volunteer with Young Life for twenty years. When I started Young Life in Saratoga, Dave agreed to be my committee chairman. He helped me with the strategy for growing the area and helped with the fundraising. He and I met for breakfast several times each month, and he was an incredible source of encouragement during my years in Saratoga.

I invited Dave inside. He said, "I've got something for you," as he handed me a brown paper bag. I looked in the bag and was dumbstruck. It was filled with cash and personal checks made out to me. When Dave heard I was on unpaid leave from Young Life, he wanted to help. He saw the opportunity to help me in what he knew would be a tough and stressful time. He raised money, but this time it wasn't for Young Life, it was for me and my family.

It was an incredible gift and a humbling one, generous on so many levels. It was a wonderful surprise to receive thousands of dollars from dozens of people who wanted to help me and let me know they cared about me and my family. In a moment of such uncertainty, adjusting to being a dad for the first time, losing my job, struggling to pay bills, Dave helped in a personal and profound way. The notes I received along with the money were so encouraging. Dave reminded me I had people in my corner, that I wasn't walking the journey alone.

Twenty-five years later, Dave's kindness still ranks as one of the most memorable moments in my life. He seized an opportunity and brought purpose to it. The impact has been enduring. You can have a lasting impact on people. You don't have to bring a bag of money, just help them with what they need. When someone in your life hits hard times, seize the opportunity to help. Remind them they aren't alone on the journey. Years from now they will remember, and maybe they'll write about you in their book.

Everyday people seizing the opportunities in front of them and filling them with purpose. There are no special skills needed or requirements. All it takes is a watchful eye to notice those in need around you and the willingness to act. Every day, everywhere, there are opportunities you could fill with purpose. The only question is whether you will take notice and take action. Your story will be better if you do.

21

PURPOSE AT WORK

A life of purpose must take into account what we do for a living. We spend so many waking hours at work, and many see work as the obstacle that prevents them from pursuing the life they want to be living. How does work fit into an extraordinary life?

Rather than delve into the well-debated question, Should I pursue passion or practicality? I would look at work from a fresh point of view. Some will pursue their passion and thrive. Others will pursue it and fail. Some will play it safe and choose a practical profession and find both fulfillment and happiness. Others will only find misery. Like everything else in life, how you view your work is subjective. Two people looking at the same circumstances can see the situation in altogether different ways. Looking for the positive in every situation is always a superb place to start.

I look at work from a practical point of view. Most people have to work. We have jobs because we need money to provide for our needs. It's as simple as that. Some jobs are better than others, but that's no different from all other aspects of life. Some are born in prosperous countries while others in war-torn nations. Some will have loving families and others will have families that neglect and ignore. If you compare your circumstances to those of others, in any aspect of your life, you've already lost. Living the life you want to live has nothing to do with how anyone else is living. The only question is, can you create a better life for yourself tomorrow than you are living today? Work plays a significant part in that equation.

I find it helpful to start from a place of practical appreciation. The more we can appreciate the positives of our current circumstances, the better life will be. You may not have the perfect job, but the unemployed person who has been searching for work, month after month, would be grateful for the one you've got. We compare the jobs we have to people who have the jobs we wish we had. We would be better off comparing ourselves to people doing jobs we would never want, or to those with no work at all. It's a blessing to have a job, and having one is easy to take for granted.

The Great Depression began on October 24, 1929, when the stock market crashed and millions of people lost all their money. The Great Depression devastated the United States economy from 1929 to 1939. Twenty percent of the workforce was unemployed. Banks were failing. Bread lines, soup kitchens, and shantytowns sprang up across the country as the number of homeless people grew.[1] Severe drought and dust storms ravaged the Midwest, wiping out crops and killing livestock. Millions of people migrated west in search of work.

There are several poignant photographs from that time

that bring instant clarity and perspective on what it means to suffer through hard times. Unemployed men lined up around the block hoping for a warm meal at a soup kitchen. Desperate families unable to feed their kids posting signs saying, "Children for sale. Inquire within." How hopeless must you be to give up your children?

The unemployed moved town to town in search of work. They were greeted by billboards saying, "Jobless men keep going. We can't take care of our own." These were signs posted by the chamber of commerce.

Children walked the streets holding signs saying, "Why can't you give my dad a job?" And men walked the streets wearing sandwich board signs asking for a chance to work. One famous picture shows a man wearing a sign that reads, "I know 3 trades. I speak 3 languages. Fought for 3 years. Have 3 children and no work for 3 months but I only want one job."[2] You can feel the despair and desperation. Against this backdrop, the vast majority of us are in situations that can't compare in the slightest. We complain about not getting enough recognition from a demanding boss. The people in the depression were trying to survive and feed their hungry children. Fifteen million people, a quarter of the eligible workforce, would have given anything for the job you have right now.

The purpose of work is to provide. If you have a job, be grateful. But your job also plays several important additional roles. As you design the life you want to live, resistance and struggle are key components. There is no light without darkness, and we appreciate triumph only after the struggle. If I handed you everything you wanted with no effort required, the value and significance would disappear. No fantastic story is told where everything is easy: "Once upon a time, there was a lucky couple who lived the perfect life. They had everything they desired, they enjoyed every day and lived happily ever after." We celebrate stories of perseverance and determination. We admire people who overcome hardship and beat the odds. If we want to live a remarkable story with our lives, there must be resistance and challenge.

In the 1990s, scientists completed construction of a research facility called Biosphere 2 in Arizona. The purpose was to determine whether scientists could create a self-sustaining, enclosed ecosystem that would support human life. They were hoping to prove they could build colonies that could support mankind on the moon.

Biosphere 2 sprawled across three acres that contained dedicated areas of tropical rain forest, desert, ocean with coral reef, savanna grassland, wetlands, and an agricultural area. A crew entered the biosphere as part of the experiment to see if the ecosystem could produce all the components to sustain healthy living. They encountered many issues and determined that they could not create a self-sustaining closed ecosystem. But there were some significant scientific discoveries.

Scientists found that the trees in Biosphere 2 grew faster than was typical, but the trees would fall over before they could mature. Researchers came to determine that it was the lack of wind inside the biosphere that caused the issue. They realized that trees in the wild were in constant motion, swaying in the wind. This strengthened the roots, trunk, and branches. The stress put on the trees by the wind was a necessary element in helping the trees mature. Without that stress, the trees collapsed under their own weight because they lacked the strength to hold themselves up.[3]

Just as the trees needed the stress of the wind to help them grow strong, we need resistance pressing on us to help us develop and mature. Without it, we too collapse under the weight of life's challenges. Work is one element of wind in our lives. It forces us to bend and adapt to other people and their agendas. There are conflicts and constraints, disappointments and deadlines. They all serve as the winds and storms that help strengthen and develop us into mature people.

Work, with all its difficulties and demands, provides a place for you to accomplish something, and we all want to accomplish something with our lives. Work plays a crucial role in shaping you into the person you need to become to live the extraordinary life you hope to live.

A Place for Purpose

After six years working for Young Life, I got a job at a small, high tech startup called GolfPro International, a company developing robotic caddies for the golf industry. I was leading human resources, something I knew nothing about. My then father-in-law introduced me to the CEO, and I was grateful for the opportunity. Little did I know, I would remain in human resources for the next two decades.

My learning curve was fast and steep. I got educated by taking people to lunch and asking a thousand questions. I met people at their office hoping I could look around and inquire about what I was seeing. I borrowed everything I could get my hands on and studied it all. I hoped that I would learn enough so I wouldn't embarrass myself or reveal my complete lack of HR knowledge.

People were beyond gracious. I borrowed market research, compensation studies, policy handbooks, all things I was putting in place at GolfPro International. When I needed to put together a compensation plan, the industry survey data was too generic. So I asked three CFOs from other companies if they would share with me their actual payroll files so I could get a sense of how real salary information aligned with the survey data. All three said yes. I'm still struck with the amount of trust they had in me to share such sensitive information. But I appreciated their help.

Ron, the CEO of GolfPro, asked me to come to his office one evening. Earlier in the day he spoke with the head of engineering. Ron told me, "I thought you'd get a kick out of this. I was meeting with Bob today, and he told me you were the best HR guy he's ever worked with. I was so tempted to tell him you had no clue what you were doing!" He then told me I was doing an outstanding job, and he knew that someday, I would be one of the top HR people in the Silicon Valley. His encouragement meant a lot, as did his confidence in me. To this day, I'm so appreciative for his willingness to take a chance on me. It changed my career and financial future.

I've had a wonderful career working for some of the best companies in the world. I too have taken a chance on people without a traditional background. Some of them have turned out to be the best hires I've ever made. I'm intentional about mentoring people trying to figure out their career because I remember how important it was for me to have someone help me figure it out. I work hard to develop the people on my team so they develop exceptional skills that will help them thrive for the rest of their careers. And my job has changed into one where I now focus on helping people develop the skills they need to navigate life and do the best work in their careers.

I have filled my career with moments of purpose, some unexpected and some pursued. I've had the privilege of giving wings to other people's dreams and walking with them during some difficult days. Too many people have allowed themselves to dread work. That's a shame. I see it as the arena in which I get to pursue purpose with wonderful people. You will work for decades. Imagine all you can do in that time if you use it as a place of purpose, a place to thrive, not merely something you endure.

PART IV

CLOSING THE GAP

Lots of people know what to do, but few people actually do what they know. Knowing is not enough! You must take action.

—Tony Robbins

22

DO IT RESPONSIBLY

W hether you ever live the life you've imagined will depend on whether you move from thinking to doing. Benjamin Disraeli said, "Action may not always bring happiness; but there is no happiness without action." Taking action may not bring you everything you want in life, but your life will never be all you want it to be without taking action.

While we dream and plan, life goes on. The life you've imagined and the life you are living may be miles apart, but you can close the gap by taking the right actions. In this section we will explore the actions you can take that will allow you to enjoy the life you want to live.

Money won't make you happy. But the lack of it can make you miserable. Too many people waste their lives chasing wealth, and no matter how much they accumulate, it's not enough. There's nothing wrong with having money, but make sure you don't miss the best parts of life pursuing it.

As you create the life you want, money is a part of the equation. If you desire to travel the world and see amazing places in faraway lands, you need to have the financial means to afford it. If your perfect life includes daring adventures and fine dining, you don't want a lack of money to be what's holding you back.

How much money you need only you can decide, but it's a slippery slope. John D. Rockefeller was the first billionaire in the United States and the wealthiest person in the world. A reporter once asked him how much money was enough. Rockefeller's response? "Just a little bit more."[1]

This sums up how many people think about money. To have enough, they need just a little more. A little more to be secure. A little more to be content. A little more to be happy. Seneca, a Roman philosopher, said, "It is not the man who has too little, but the man who craves more, who is poor." Be careful in your pursuit of just a little bit more.

I've seen this phenomenon firsthand. I know several people who set out to become millionaires, only to realize that $1 million wasn't enough. They set their sights on $2 million, then $4 million. As they achieved each milestone, their needs grew larger. Each time the response was the same. Now that they were more educated about financial matters, they realized their initial goals were too low. They needed just a little more . . .

Lao Tzu said, "Be content with what you have; rejoice in the way things are. When you realize there is nothing lacking, the whole world belongs to you." Life would be much simpler if we determined today that what we have is enough.

As you think about strategies for living your best life, recognize that being content with what you have gets you a long way toward living the life you want to live. Learning how to handle money helps you improve things from there.

Living your best life requires some financial common sense and discipline. When your finances are out of control, they will always be a weight around your neck hindering you from living the life you want to live. If you don't understand financial matters like investing and budgeting, do yourself a favor and learn. Get disciplined with your finances or you will jeopardize your chances of being able to do all you want to do in life. There are thousands of excellent books on money. Invest the time to become knowledgeable on the subject. Think of it as an investment in the life you want to live.

Financial matters can get complicated if you wander into Wall Street, stocks and bonds, derivatives, real estate, investing, etc. Forget all that. Simplify. The most rudimentary knowledge can get you moving in the right direction and set you up for financial freedom. First, make money. Second, spend less than you make. Third, set money aside without fail. Fourth, make the money you save work for you. By investing well, your money will grow. If you follow these four rules, always, you'll put yourself in a position to have the financial means necessary to do what you want to do.

Money won't make your problems go away, and it won't make you happy. There are plenty of miserable rich people with lots of problems. It's an excellent reminder that money isn't everything. But living in dire straits, always worried about paying the bills, won't give you the freedom you need to enjoy life. Take care of the basics. At the very least, follow the four financial steps I've noted until you get more educated. Learn about financial matters so a lack of money doesn't limit your ability to live the life of your dreams.

23

DO IT CONSISTENTLY

W hen James Harrison was fourteen years old, he needed to have a lung removed. The operation kept him in the hospital for three months. During the surgery, James received several blood transfusions to keep him alive, almost two gallons of blood. After the surgery, James's father explained that the blood transfusions that saved him came from strangers who had donated their blood. James decided he would repay the favor someday.

When James turned eighteen, he made good on his promise. He went to the blood bank and made his first donation. They discovered his blood contained rare antibodies that could fight rhesus disease, a disease in pregnant women where the mother's blood attacks the blood cells of her unborn child. Rhesus disease can cause miscarriage, stillbirths, brain damage, and premature death for newborns. Doctors realized that Harrison's blood could save the lives of the many babies who were dying because of rhesus each year.

Knowing his blood could help mothers and babies, James

committed to donating blood again. From the age of eighteen until he was eighty-one, over six decades, James showed up every few weeks and donated his blood. All said, he donated blood 1,173 times! He would have given more, but people in Australia can't donate blood past the age of eighty-one.

On his final donation, the staff at the blood bank brought in half a dozen women and their babies. James Harrison's blood had been used to save them all. They thanked him for his generosity and noted that those six babies were just a few of the 2.4 million babies saved by Harrison's blood donations.[1]

James Harrison received the Medal of the Order of Australia for his generosity. He's known as the Man with the Golden Arm. Harrison said, "It becomes quite humbling when they say, 'Oh you've done this or you've done that or you're a hero.' . . . It's something I can do. It's one of my talents, probably my only talent, is that I can be a blood donor."[2]

An interesting side note, Harrison hates needles.[3] He showed up 1,173 times to do something he hated doing. Why? He wanted to give back. What makes it extraordinary is not that he gave blood that saved lives, it's that he showed up for over sixty years. The consistency of his actions makes his story remarkable.

If you want to affect the world, your family, the life you live, then consistency is an important part of the equation. The wonderful news is that consistency is within your control. At the end of your life, people may remember you for something you did once or twice. But they will definitely remember you if you did something meaningful over a lengthy period.

An extraordinary life requires action and consistency. Throughout this book we've explored possibilities for living a remarkable life, but without taking action, your best life will remain unlived, your best stories left untold.

What actions, if repeated with consistency, could change your life for the better? If you want to live the life you've imagined, it will require discipline. It will also require you to apply the power of habits in your life.

24

DO IT HABITUALLY

The ability to take consistent action is essential to living the life we want to live. At the very least, we have to stop taking steps that move us farther away from our goals. Direction and consistency are key components of success.

Too many people have predetermined that they don't have the discipline or willpower to do what it takes to move from where they are to where they'd like to be. And those people are wrong. It's not a question of whether you can make the changes, it's a question of whether you are approaching the change in an intelligent and effective manner.

F. Matthias Alexander said, "People do not decide their futures, they decide their habits and their habits decide their futures." When I first read his statement, I disagreed. My experience told me that setting goals was the catalyst that made everything else possible, and without setting goals, success was unlikely. I still believe there is undeniable power in setting goals, but I agree with Alexander. Habits are the means by which you can bring your goals to life. Dreams and goals without the habits to move you to action will amount to nothing.

A study from Duke University found that over 40 percent of our daily actions are because of habits and not based on decisions we make.[1] That could be good news, or bad, depending on what your habits are. If 40 percent of your actions are automatic, and those actions are moving you away from the life you want, that won't work out so well. Achieving your goals will feel like pushing a boulder up a hill.

There is hope. Charles Duhigg, in his book *The Power of Habit*, notes, "Habits are powerful, but delicate. They can emerge outside our consciousness, or can be deliberately designed."[2] You can decide the habits you want and put them to work for you. We may have formed a few habits (probably bad ones) unconsciously, but habits can also be intentionally and deliberately designed and implemented. If you can make the habitual 40 percent of your day work for you, the life you want to live is within reach. The question is, how do we design the habits we want to have?

There are several excellent books dedicated to creating habits. Two I recommend are *Atomic Habits* by James Clear and *The Power of Habit* by Charles Duhigg. What I thought would be a boring topic turned out to be both interesting and relevant. Both books go into detail on the science of habits, what works and what doesn't. They outline practical strategies for creating habits that can affect your life. Read them. They will help you create the life you want to live.

There are many useful strategies in both books, but if I could boil it down, there are two key approaches to success.

First, make your good habits easy to achieve. And second, make your bad habits difficult to continue. Gravity is a powerful force. Do everything possible to reduce friction and remove the obstacles that often entangle us. Eliminate what keeps you from taking the actions you want to take. And to get rid of destructive behaviors, put obstacles in the way to prevent you from taking the actions you've decided aren't helping you live the life you want. Make your habitual 40 percent work to your advantage.

Make It Difficult

When Ronan Byrne was a student at the Dublin Institute of Technology in Ireland, he found himself conflicted. He wanted to be healthy and in shape, but he also wanted to binge-watch hours of Netflix. It wasn't much of a contest. Netflix was winning, hands down. But rather than concede defeat, Ronan applied the basic rules of habits. He decided he needed to make his binge-watching more difficult and his exercise a part of his routine.

Ronan looked for a way to bring the two competing activities together, a way to increase his exercise and allow him to continue watching Netflix. His solution? Cycflix, something Ronan called exercise-powered entertainment.[3]

Cycflix was a system Byrne designed to connect his television with a stationary bicycle. He programmed the system so that Netflix would play only if the pedal speed of the stationary bike maintained a predetermined pace. If the RPMs of the bike fell below the set threshold, Netflix would pause until the speed increased accordingly. Ronan's creative approach combined the two essential elements of successful habit-setting. He made the undesired activity more difficult, and he made his desired activity a part of his normal routine. Now his binge-watching of Netflix would make him exercise and help get him in better shape.

Make It Easy

When I was thinking about my life and all I wanted to do, I put running a marathon on my bucket list. Not because I enjoy running. I hate it. But the progress required to achieve the goal intrigued me. Sports always came easy for me, but I knew that if someone offered me $1 million to run 26.2 miles, I wouldn't have been able to do it. I wanted to experience what it was like to do the work necessary to make the impossible possible.

Over the years, I ran very little, and never more than a few miles. Running a marathon was inconceivable. It exhausted me to run for thirty minutes, let alone the hours required to run over twenty-six miles. I knew it wouldn't happen without intentional commitment and effort. I needed to put the systems in place that would enable me to reach my goal.

I started researching marathon training, and most of the literature had one piece of advice I hadn't considered. I needed to get a training partner to share the journey. It's too easy to skip training days because more often than not, you won't feel like going. But if you know there is someone waiting outside for you, there's a much higher likelihood that you will drag yourself out of bed and hit the road.

I called my friend Derek and let him know that running a marathon was in his future. He'd never run a marathon either, but he was up for it. We trained together for six months. Every Saturday we met up to do our long runs together. And then on a cold, blustery day in San Francisco, we lined up on the Sausalito side of the Golden Gate Bridge and embarked on an incredible journey through 26.2 miles of San Francisco scenery. It was an amazing experience, and one I know I wouldn't have accomplished without Derek. A training partner was the missing ingredient for me in that endeavor. I succeeded because I made it more difficult to skip out on the training when I knew Derek was waiting for me to show up.

If you want to live the life you have imagined, maybe you need a training partner or a creative solution to help you exercise more. You may need to make some of your habits more difficult to achieve, and the desirable ones more accessible. To close the gap between the life you have and the life you want, it's imperative that you create the systems that will enable you to succeed. You will need systems that will help you take actions that move you toward your desired life.

James Clear notes, "You do not rise to the level of your goals. You fall to the level of your systems."[4] Ronan Byrne had a goal to exercise more, but that wasn't enough. It wasn't until he put a system in place that he found success. Once you figure out what you want to achieve in your life, create the habits that will take you where you want to go. Take the time to put in place the systems that will help you achieve your goals.

25

DO IT DESPITE THE DIFFICULTIES

K eith Jarrett is an American jazz pianist. He's also a perfectionist. Sometimes he hands out cough drops to the audience to ensure that no one coughs during his performances. He likes things a certain way.

In 1975, Jarrett embarked on a twenty-date tour through Europe. He was performing solo, improvised concerts. Each concert was its own unique experience, and for Jarrett, each was exhausting. He played concerts every other day so he would have time to recuperate between shows. Despite these precautions, Jarrett was plagued with chronic back issues and was having trouble sleeping. But he pressed on, counting down his remaining shows. Then the invitation came.

In Cologne, Germany, there is a magnificent venue called the Koln Opera House. No jazz musician had ever performed a concert in the beautiful theater. Vera Brandes, a determined seventeen-year-old jazz enthusiast, was hoping to change that and make history. She convinced the Koln Opera House to allow a jazz concert, and now she was calling Keith Jarrett asking him to perform. The only date available for the performance was January 24 at 11:00 p.m. The late hour was because the jazz concert would happen after an opera performance taking place earlier that evening. Jarrett intended January 24 to be a rest day, but it was a once-in-a-lifetime opportunity to be the first jazz performer at the Koln Opera House, so he altered his plans and agreed to play.

Jarrett sent Brandes the specifications of the equipment he needed, most importantly, a Bösendorfer 290 Imperial Concert Grand piano. He planned to arrive in the afternoon, look over the venue, get something to eat, and then return to perform. Jarrett played a show in Zurich the night before, so he had a 350-mile drive to get to Cologne. Not the day of rest his tired body needed.

When Jarrett arrived, he walked through the opera house imagining the acoustics of the grand hall and the audience that would hear him play later that evening. Everything was perfect until he saw the piano. There was no nine-foot Bösendorfer 290 Imperial Concert Grand piano. Instead, there was a dilapidated half-sized piano sitting on the stage.

It got worse. The piano was terribly out of tune. Not all the keys worked, and the sustain pedal was broken. The black keys in the middle of the keyboard were sticky, and the tone of the instrument was more akin to a tinny harpsichord than a rich, deep-toned grand piano. For the perfectionist Jarrett, the piano was unplayable. He told Vera Brandes the show was off.

Vera imagined the 1,400 customers who would show up at 11:00 p.m. for the sold-out show, disappointed and angry. She ran after Jarrett, who was already in his car ready to leave. Standing in the pouring rain, Vera pleaded with Jarrett to reconsider. She said she would do whatever was possible to remedy the piano situation. Maybe it was the pleading. Maybe the tears. But Jarrett relented and agreed to play the show. He left for dinner and Vera set about trying to find a better piano.

Jarrett and his team went to an Italian restaurant for dinner. The restaurant was unbearably hot; the service was slow, and the food was bad. For the tired pianist with an aching back, the miserable dining experience wasn't helping.

Meanwhile, Vera Brandes was trying to remedy the unplayable piano. She found a nine-foot Bösendorfer 290 Imperial Concert Grand piano, but the moving company had already packed up and gone home. She rounded up a group of friends, thinking they would push the grand piano through the streets of Cologne to get it to the Opera House. They abandoned that idea once they realized they would ruin the piano by bouncing it through the streets in the rain. The best Vera could do was get someone to tune the old piano. Hours later, it was in tune as much as it could be, but the keys that hadn't been working still didn't, the keys that were sticky were still stuck, the broken sustain pedal was still not working, and the tone of the piano still lacked depth, richness, and volume.

When Jarrett arrived, Brandes explained her failed efforts to get the concert piano, and the hours spent tuning the one on stage. This was as good as it would get, which wasn't good at all. Keith spoke to his manager and asked that he record the performance. He figured he could share it with other concert promoters as a not-so-subtle warning on the disappointing results they could expect if they ever provided the wrong equipment or a bad piano.[1]

The opera performance before Jarrett's show ran late. The crowd was still filing in well past the intended 11:00 p.m. start time. Jarrett took the stage at 11:30 to face the sold-out crowd. Exhausted already, he began. He played the jangly, flawed piano. As Jarrett was improvising the entire performance, he set about getting to know the limitations of the instrument. He avoided the keys that didn't work. Without a working sustain pedal he played with a punctuated style, while pounding the lower register of keys to coerce more sound from the worn-out strings. For more than an hour, Jarrett bent over the piano, laboring and grunting, willing the old piano to cooperate with the music he was trying to play. And somehow, despite the broken-down piano and exhausted body of the pianist, something magical happened.

Jarrett's Koln concert at the opera house became legendary. He released the recording of the performance, and it became the bestselling jazz piano album of all time, with over four million sold.[2] The night he expected to be a disaster turned out to be the high point in Keith Jarrett's career, one he almost walked away from because the circumstances were so difficult.

We are all guaranteed to encounter difficulties in life. Some situations will feel so daunting we'll want to get in the car and leave them behind. But there's a lesson we can take from Keith Jarrett and his incredible performance at the opera house. Sometimes the difficulties will be the very reason something extraordinary happens.

The music Jarrett played that cold, rainy night in Germany never would have happened if he had performed the opera house show on a perfect nine-foot Bösendorfer 290 Imperial Concert Grand piano as he intended. The reason the performance was extraordinary is that he had to adapt to all the flaws of the dilapidated piano. He had to avoid playing notes he was accustomed to playing. He had to pound harder than usual to coax more sound from the worn-out lower-register notes. Jarrett had to change his style to overcome the lack of sustain due to the broken pedal. And all those adjustments happened only because he had to overcome the glaring deficiencies of a broken-down piano. The difficulties that night in Cologne are the reason the performance came out as it did.[3] Remarkable and extraordinary.

Nobody welcomes difficulties into their life. We choose the path of least resistance. We want our plans to work out as we imagined. And so we turn away from difficulties. Just like Jarrett, we get in the car and declare this part or that part of life "unplayable." But what if we learned to avoid the sticky keys and pound a little harder than normal to get more out of a bad situation? Like it or not, we are most shaped and molded in the hard times. If we avoid the challenges, we miss the growth.

To close the gap that exists between the life you have and the life you want, lean into the difficulties. Play the broken-down pianos that life puts on your stage. You've got a remarkable performance in you that will only come out if you push through the challenges. Get out of the car, go back on stage, and play. That's where your best life is. On the stage. In the arena. Down in the dust of difficulty. It shocked Keith Jarrett to see his concert on a dilapidated piano become the bestselling jazz piano album. We may be shocked as well to find our greatest moments on the other side of our difficulties.

26

DO WHAT YOU CAN

R obert Leibowitz didn't want to wait any longer. It had been over four years, and nothing had changed. So he took matters into his own hands. His plan was far from perfect. It was almost ridiculous. But somehow, it worked.

Leibowitz had been suffering with kidney disease since he was twelve years old. He was now sixty. Over the years, his condition had grown worse. Four years earlier, Leibowitz went on the waiting list to receive a kidney transplant. So far, nothing. Leibowitz now required kidney dialysis, a treatment that filters blood and removes toxins failing kidneys can't remove. Each treatment lasts four hours, and Robert was having treatments three times a week. He decided he would not sit back and wait any longer. He was ready to take action.

In his autobiography, Teddy Roosevelt notes the philosophy of Squire Bill Widener, "Do what you can, with what you've got, where you are." It was in this spirit that Robert Leibowitz decided he would do what he could. He was taking his five kids on a nine-day trip to Disney World.

Leibowitz spent $30 to have a custom T-shirt printed with a message on the front and the back:

In Need Of Kidney
O Positive
Call
917-597-2651

Leibowitz wore his custom T-shirt all nine days at Disney World. Rocio Sandoval saw Leibowitz with his family and noticed his T-shirt. She took a picture and posted it on her Facebook page. Within twenty-four hours, over 33,000 people shared Sandoval's picture of Leibowitz. The next week another 90,000 people shared her post. Leibowitz started getting texts, Facebook messages, and phone calls. Over three hundred of them. Some people wanted to see if it was real, if someone was crazy enough to put his real phone number on a T-shirt. But one call was from a man named Richie Sully, and Richie wanted to help.

To be a living kidney donor, a potential donor needs to go through a series of tests to determine whether the kidney is suitable. Richie completed the tests, and his kidney was an excellent match for Robert. When asked why he would undergo surgery to give one of his kidneys to a stranger, Sully said, "A guy needs this to live, and I have an extra one." He added, "The way I was raised, if someone needs help you give it to them."[1]

Four months later, Leibowitz and Sully checked into New York-Presbyterian Hospital, where doctors removed one of Richie Sully's healthy kidneys and transplanted it into Robert Leibowitz. The surgery was a success. Richie Sully met a stranger, helped save his life, and five kids still had their dad because of it.[2]

At first, Richie Sully wanted to remain anonymous about his part in Robert Leibowitz's story. But he realized that by sharing he could raise awareness of live kidney donations and perhaps inspire someone else to donate and save a life. He said, "I didn't even know that was a thing until all this happened. . . . I hope I can help other people who are on the waiting list." Richie Sully stepped up and seized the opportunity to help a man in need, and along the way he found a purpose personal to him.

How do you close the gap between the life you have and the life you want? You do what Robert Leibowitz did, what Rocio Sandoval did, and what Richie Sully did. Leibowitz didn't sit back and wait any longer. He took action. He did what he could, with what he had, from where he was.

Rocio Sandoval also took action. She empathized with a man wanting to spend more time with his kids. As a mother, she could understand how hard it would be, fighting for your life, needing to rely on the kindness of a stranger. So she took a picture, and she posted it on Facebook.

The story would end there if it weren't for the 120,000 people who shared the picture. Each one of them played a part in the story. One of those people told Richie Sully about a post she had read on Facebook. And then there is Richie. We can adopt his mindset. When someone needs help, you help them.

In six months, three strangers' lives became intertwined, and all of them are better for it. Life can change in an instant. Six months from now, your life could differ greatly from what it is today. Maybe you will find an opportunity and do something like Richie Sully did. Those are the actions that will help you make the most of your one wild and precious life.

A life of purpose requires a little humanity, and it requires some selfless actions. You don't have to change the world. Just do what you can, with what you've got, wherever you are. Who knows, maybe your $30 T-shirt idea will save somebody's life. Try it.

27

DO IT WITH DETERMINATION

Teddy Roosevelt was a man of courage and action, determined to live life to the fullest. Mount Rushmore bears his image, tucked between the faces of Thomas Jefferson and Abraham Lincoln. He is the youngest president of the United States, and historians consider him one of the top five presidents in history. He took expeditions through the Amazon, led the Rough Riders in the Spanish-American War, and won a Nobel Peace Prize. He was a man of action and courage, but his journey was anything but easy.

Roosevelt was sick and frail as a child. Asthma limited his activity, but he worked hard and exercised strenuously to overcome his frailty. He attended Harvard, where he met Alice Hathaway Lee. He was smitten from the start. His diary entry after they first met said, "As long as I live, I shall never forget how sweetly she looked, and how prettily she greeted me."[1] Teddy and Alice got engaged on Valentine's Day and married eight months later. Roosevelt went to Columbia Law

School but dropped out after one year to pursue local politics in New York.

Four years into their marriage, Teddy and Alice were expecting their first child. Roosevelt was a New York State Assemblyman and working on legislation when he received a telegram summoning him home. Alice had delivered a baby girl and Teddy's mother was ill. Roosevelt left Albany for Manhattan, and by the time he reached home, his life would never be the same.

Roosevelt entered to find his mother burning up with a fever. Upstairs, Alice was barely conscious as her kidneys were failing. Within hours, Roosevelt met his two-day-old daughter, his mother died, and so did his beautiful wife Alice shortly after. It was February 14, the anniversary of Teddy and Alice's engagement. In his diary, Roosevelt drew a large "X" and wrote, "The light has gone out of my life."[2]

It devastated Roosevelt. After the funerals, he left his daughter, named Alice after her mother, with his sister and headed West for the Black Hills of South Dakota. For the next few years he hid on a ranch away from civilization, working as a cattle rancher and sheriff. He spent his time reading and writing about history. When a blizzard wiped out his herd, Roosevelt decided it was time to head back to New York and rejoin his now three-year-old daughter.

Teddy went back into politics. He remarried and had five more children. He became vice president of the United States to President McKinley. McKinley died six months later at the hand of an assassin, and forty-two-year-old Theodore Roosevelt became president of the United States. He served the remaining three years of McKinley's term and then won reelection to serve four more years. Four years later, unhappy with the job his successor William Howard Taft was doing, Roosevelt ran for a third term.

Teddy brought his usual energy and zeal to the campaign trail. One evening he was in Milwaukee, Wisconsin, to deliver a campaign speech. He stepped out of his hotel to go to the event and a saloon owner named John Schrank pulled a revolver from his coat and shot Roosevelt in the chest from five feet away. Remarkably, Roosevelt had his fifty-page speech folded in the breast pocket of his jacket, next to his metal eyeglass case. The bullet went through both before entering Roosevelt. The crowd tackled Schrank and hauled him off to jail. They tried to get Roosevelt to a hospital, but he refused, insisting that he would first deliver his speech.

Roosevelt took the stage and asked the crowd for silence. He told them someone had just shot him, even opening his coat to reveal his blood-stained shirt. He showed the bullet-pierced speech and eyeglass holder and explained that his voice was weak but he would give a brief speech because he had important things to say. Roosevelt delivered an eighty-four-minute speech before heading to the hospital. The doctors determined it was too risky to remove the bullet lodged in his ribs, so they left the bullet in Roosevelt, where it stayed the rest of his life.[3]

Despite his frailty as a child and heartbreak as an adult, Teddy Roosevelt lived life on his terms. He let nothing stand in his way, not even a bullet in his chest. To live the life you want to live, that's the commitment and determination you need to have. You have one chance to get it right. Whatever limitations you have, whatever heartbreak you've suffered, do not let it deter you from pursuing life with every ounce of determination you can muster.

In his book *Walden*, Henry David Thoreau wrote, "If one advances confidently in the direction of his dreams, and endeavors to live the life which he has imagined, he will meet with a success unexpected in common hours." Don't wait. Advance toward the life you want. Walk in the direction of your dreams, and commit with determination to live the life you have imagined. The success you find will be a life worth living, a life that looks back without regret. A life with meaning. The life you want to live.

28

DO IT UNTIL

Creating the life you want will be the most challenging endeavor you undertake. You will fail, wishes won't come true. But don't lose hope. Failure is an expected part of the journey, and it doesn't mean you won't ultimately accomplish what you set out to do. Success, after repeated failures, can be the sweetest victory of all. And if anyone knows this, it's Diana Nyad.

Diana grew up in the water. She loved swimming. She was a state champion swimmer in high school and became an ultra-distance swimmer in college. At twenty-six, she attempted the twenty-eight-mile swim around the island of Manhattan. She swam for eight hours then had to be pulled from the East River in the middle of the night, exhausted and trembling. She got sick from swimming in the polluted water, but as soon as she was feeling better, she tried again. On her second attempt she completed the twenty-eight-mile swim in seven hours and fifty-seven minutes, breaking a four-decades-old record.

When Diana was twenty-eight, she attempted what most believed was impossible. She set out to swim from Cuba to Florida, a distance of 110 miles through shark-infested waters. Nyad encountered rough seas and currents that pushed her so far off course she had to abandon her attempt 79 miles into the swim. She'd been in the water for forty-two hours.

On her thirtieth birthday, Diana entered what she believed would be her last competitive swim. She swam 102 miles from the Bahamas to Florida in twenty-seven and a half hours, setting a world record for open ocean swimming. Diana retired and didn't swim again. Until.

Thirty years later, Diana's mother died at eighty-two. Diana reflected on her own life, what she had accomplished, and what she still wanted to do with her remaining years. She realized, "I just didn't want to have any regrets. I kept on thinking about all the things in my life I could have done differently. My mother had died at 82 and I realized I might only have 22 years left and I just wanted to make sure I really lived them."[1] One regret in particular kept coming to mind. The unfinished business of Cuba.

Diana contemplated what it would take to complete the swim from Cuba to Florida. Her first attempt, when she was twenty-eight years old, had failed. It seemed beyond reason to believe she could succeed now, in her sixties, at a challenge so daunting she couldn't achieve it when she was in her prime. Was it crazy to try? Was it even possible? Diana decided to find out.

Thirty-one years after retiring from marathon swimming, Diana Nyad started training. For eighteen months she reconditioned her body to prepare for the grueling challenge ahead. Two weeks before her sixty-second birthday, Nyad entered the waters near Havana, Cuba, and started swimming for the shores of America. A few hours in, her shoulder hurt badly. She pressed on through the strong current for twenty-nine hours. She began having trouble breathing as she suffered an asthma attack. Her attempt was over. But not her dream or her will to accomplish it.

Six and a half weeks later, Nyad eased into the Cuban waters for her third attempt. She swam for sixty-seven miles, over forty-one hours, but her body took a beating along the way. Jellyfish, Portuguese man-of-war, and the deadliest of all, the box jellyfish, stung Nyad multiple times. Her support team pulled her from the water. She had failed a third time. Nyad was disappointed, but not defeated. She would be back.

One year later, a week before her sixty-third birthday, Diana set out for the fourth time to achieve her dream, the 110-mile swim from Cuba to Florida. It was not to be. She encountered storms and rough seas, and more jellyfish. With her tongue and lips swollen, her crew once again had to pull her from the water. She'd been swimming for over fifty hours and had made it only halfway to Florida. But Nyad wasn't giving up. She was still pursuing the life she wanted to live. For Diana Nyad it was clear, "Instead of staying on the couch for a lifetime and letting this precious time go by, why not be bold, be fiercely bold and go out and chase your dreams?"[2]

The chase would continue a year later, a few weeks after her sixty-fourth birthday. On August 31, Diana Nyad left the shores of Cuba for her fifth attempt to reach Florida. She wore a thin body suit, and a silicone face mask designed to help protect her from the deadly jellyfish. She had support boats nearby with her team of medics, navigators, and shark divers. Diana had a team of kayakers who paddled close, dragging an electronic device emitting an electromagnetic field to ward off sharks. She had a guide boat that dragged a guideline that hovered a few feet under the water so she could more easily follow the guide boat. And this time Diana got lucky.

Nyad didn't encounter the jellyfish that had been so detrimental during her previous attempts. She found calm waters and a favorable current, so she stayed on course. Her greatest struggle was with the new silicone mask she wore for protection. It chafed and created sores, and it caused her to swallow a lot of sea water, making her vomit through much of the swim. Still, she pressed on, undeterred.

She swam for fifty-three hours, sunburned, swollen, and seasick. And after four failed and painful attempts, Diana Nyad reached the shores of Florida, emerging from the water to cheering fans. Thirty-four years after her first attempt, Diana had accomplished her greatest challenge and biggest dream.[3]

Nyad's accomplishment is staggering, something none of us will ever attempt. But the lesson is in the attempts, not in the accomplishment. As she reflected on her life, her overriding thought was that she wanted to make sure she lived her life to the fullest. She didn't want to waste her one wild and precious life. So she went after the challenge she was most passionate about. And she didn't quit pursuing it until she achieved her goal. Jim Rohn answers the question we've all asked ourselves, "How long should you try? Until."

Is there one thing above all others that stirs your soul and lingers inside your mind? Try. Have you already attempted it and failed? Try again. As Nyad said, don't settle for sitting on the couch and letting precious time go by. Be fiercely bold and go chase your dreams.

To close the gap between the life you have and the life you want, take action and pursue the moments you most believe will add to the story of your life. You don't have forever. For Diana, it was seeing her mother die and having the stark realization that she might have only twenty or twenty-five years left to live. No one has the promise of another day, let alone a life of eighty years. It could all end tomorrow. All the more reason to get off the couch right now and chase your dreams. And keep chasing them until.

29

DO IT NOW

I coached high school diving for over a decade. It's a tough sport because so much of it is a mental game. Overcoming fear, convincing yourself to do things that seem illogical, like somersaulting toward the board instead of away from it. It was always interesting to see who came out to join the diving team.

There were ex-gymnasts accustomed to somersaults and flexibility. Others were the life-of-the-party types there for the thrills and the attention. And a few were the quiet, determined types who had something to prove. Of the scores of kids I coached over the years, Mike was perhaps the most interesting.

Mike was a tough kid, a loner. He was a junior and had just moved into the area, so this was his first year at the high school. Mike had long hair and tattoos. He was quiet and skinny but strong, and he didn't listen to a thing I said. He was fiercely independent and kept to himself. He was into martial arts and as far as I could tell, the other guys on the team were afraid of him.

Diving can be counterintuitive. It requires you to train your body to do things your mind isn't too excited about. Mike was stubborn, and he thought he could figure it out on his own, so he didn't really try too hard to incorporate any of the feedback I was giving him. This went on for weeks. The other divers started making progress, but Mike was more or less stuck in a rut. I had seen dozens of divers over the years who thought they knew it all, and they never did very well. Mike seemed destined for the same result.

One day Mike came out to the pool deck and asked to speak to me privately. We sat in the bleachers and he told me about his life. He was from a military family. He moved around a lot growing up, most recently from Thailand, where he had lived the past few years. He was thoughtful as he shared his story. Then he came to his point. He said he didn't trust many people. He was used to figuring things out by himself. He apologized for not listening to me over the previous weeks. He told me he needed to get to know me more before he could trust me, but having watched me work with the other divers, he was ready to begin. He told me he trusted me and would do whatever I asked him to do.

I've had many conversations with kids on the pool deck. Sometimes about diving, more often about life, trouble at home, issues at school. But I'd never had a conversation like the one I had with Mike that day. It's one thing to say you will listen to a coach, it's another thing to do it. True to his word, Mike was attentive and listened carefully and then would try exactly what I had told him to do. He was fearless, and he started making progress.

Diving involves a measure of trial and error, and things don't always turn out as expected. This usually meant a painful landing, flat on your back or stomach, or occasionally hitting the board. When that happened, most guys would procrastinate and stall, fearful of getting back on the board for another try. Mike was different. He would have a painful mishap and get out of the pool and straight back on the board to try again.

Mike's progress sped up, and he and I built a great relationship. He became one of the best divers on the team. Then report cards came out. The league had a policy that every athlete had to have a minimum grade point average of 2.0, all Cs, to be on a sports team. Mike was not doing well. His grades were well below the 2.0 standard, and the school informed us that Mike was no longer eligible to compete. It devastated Mike. He felt like he'd finally found a place he fit in and belonged, and now that was being taken away from him.

I met with the administrators, the dean, and the principal to explain Mike's unique situation. I explained his background, the progress he made, and the issues he had building trust. I thought it would be detrimental to Mike if they suspended him from the team. As much as there was empathy for Mike and his circumstances, I heard the same story again and again. The school had to follow the policy.

Mike had continued working out with the team while I was lobbying for him to remain on it, but once his suspension was final, he couldn't work out with the team any longer. It was disappointing, for Mike, for me, and for the entire team who had grown to like and admire him.

For the next few weeks Mike would show up at the

competitions to cheer on his former teammates. I would always spend time with him to see how he was doing. Not so well was the usual answer. When he was on the diving team, he had been working hard in all his classes because he knew the school required it to compete. But once they suspended him, he lost all interest in school, and his grades continued to decline. He saw school as a lost cause, and a few weeks later, Mike dropped out. He stopped by the pool deck a few weeks after that and told me he was moving. He was really struggling with all that had happened. I asked him to stay in touch and we said goodbye.

A few months went by, and I hadn't heard from Mike. Neither had any of the divers on the team. I was happy to find a letter waiting for me at home with Mike's name and return address on the envelope. It was a great letter. The kind you keep and read every once in a while to remind yourself you did something meaningful along the way.

Mike updated me on all he'd been doing over the past few months. He had moved back to Asia; he was back in school, studying martial arts and seemed to be doing well. He was very gracious and appreciative for the time he got to spend on the diving team. He told me how much he respected me and trusted me and just wanted to say thank you. Like I said, it was a great letter. He signed off saying, *If you want to— please write back.* I remember laughing and thinking, *If I want to? Of course I want to.* It was clear he was still the outcast kid that not enough people paid attention to. I put his letter on my desk to remind myself to write Mike back.

Life keeps coming, day after day. I was coaching and working and volunteering and playing in a band. Life was full, and I was purposefully on the go. A few weeks went by, and I was cleaning up my desk and found Mike's letter. I read it again and appreciated how thoughtful and kind it was. And I saw his closing remarks, *If you want to—please write back.* I put his letter on top of my stack of to-dos to remind myself to write him back soon.

Over the next several weeks, my on-the-go lifestyle continued. I swirled through life in a tornado of activity. My room would become overwhelmingly messy, and I would hit the point of necessity for tidying up. I would find Mike's letter in the growing pile of things to do, reread it, *If you want to—please write back,* then I'd place it back on top of my stack of to-dos, prominently displayed as a reminder to write back to Mike, as soon as I could.

Another month passed. I was at the pool coaching, and a few of my former divers came out to see me on the pool deck. It was fairly typical for former divers to come back to say hello. They always knew where to find me. We exchanged quick hellos and then Jason said, "Did you hear about Mike?" I said I hadn't. He said, "Mike died. He was in a street fight and someone stabbed him." The news stunned me. We reminisced about Mike, caught up on the rest of life, and they left. I wrapped up practice and went home.

I got home and went straight to my desk. I rummaged through a pile of papers and found it, Mike's letter. I opened it once again and slowly read his kind words. I reached the bottom of the letter and just stared at what may be the saddest words I've had to read, *If you want to—please write back.* All I could think was that this kid who struggled so much with trust and vulnerability may have gotten the idea I didn't want to write him back. That I didn't care enough to reply. I felt horrible.

To this day, it's one of my biggest regrets, not taking ten minutes to sit down and write a quick note back to Mike. To answer his question with a resounding, *Yes, I want to write back! So great to hear from you.* I let days and weeks and months pass by, caught up in the busyness of life. I can't recall a single thing of significance I did during those months, but I will always remember reading his letter again the day I heard he died. Staring at those haunting words, the request from a kid who had a life so much harder than most. The request I ignored from someone I cared about, someone who needed to hear they were important, who needed to hear I remembered him. *If you want to—please write back.*

Life happens. We do our best to keep up and address what's important to us. Unfortunately, it's so easy for the urgent demands of daily living to push aside the vital parts of life we ought to address. Family. Friends. People who need help or kindness or love. Words left unsaid are haunting. Apologies never spoken burrow deep into our souls and remind us of mistakes we've made.

Don't let the busyness of living derail your plans to create an extraordinary life. Don't allow yourself to buy into the false notion that you can take care of those things later. Think long and hard before putting a Mike-type letter in a pile of things to do. Right now is the only time you've got. Write now. Apologize now. Tell *someone you love them* now. Live the life you've imagined now. You might not have the chance tomorrow. *Yes, Mike. I want to write you back! So great to hear from you.*

PART V

A LIFE WORTH LIVING

Go confidently in the direction of your dreams. Live the life you've imagined.

—Henry David Thoreau

30

YOU GET TO CHOOSE

Even with the best of plans and the strongest determination, we have days when we are not living the life we want to live. Some days are just hard. Bad, disappointing, heartbreaking, devastating days. Despite our best efforts, surrounding ourselves with the right people, making sound choices, implementing healthy habits, finding moments of purpose, and choosing a positive perspective, life can be challenging. It's hard to think about living the life of your dreams in the middle of a miserable reality.

Is it realistic to believe that everyone can create a life they are excited to live? Can we all live a life of meaning and purpose, one without many regrets? What about those who live in a part of the world where a war is raging outside their door? Or where water is scarce and people don't have enough food to feed themselves or their family? Can people in these circumstances design life and live an extraordinary life?

We will all live our own lives. Some will have difficult circumstances, and others will have it easy by comparison.

But that isn't relevant. Life is not about how your life compares to someone else's. It's about whether you can improve your current circumstances in life, and whether you play a part in determining your future. You might not transform your life into something enviable and perfect, but you can shape and improve it from what it is today. Whatever your circumstances are at this moment, you can improve your life. The perfect life may not be within reach, but progress is.

Viktor Frankl was a Holocaust survivor. He was an Austrian psychiatrist who specialized in depression and suicide prevention. The Nazis shut his medical practice when they invaded Austria, and in 1942, they rounded up him and his family and sent them to concentration camps.

Frankl survived the war, but his parents, brother, and pregnant wife died in the camps.[1] He later wrote a book, *Man's Search for Meaning*, chronicling his experiences at Auschwitz and the insights he gained watching how people responded to the horrific conditions they experienced. Frankl found that inmates who could hold on to meaning in their lives, despite their terrible conditions, were the inmates more likely to survive. He realized that life has purpose and meaning, even in horrendous, painful circumstances.

Everyone has a different starting point in life. Not everyone will achieve the same outcomes. But you can find purpose and meaning. You can find hope regardless of your circumstances. Viktor Frankl found that "everything can be taken from a man but one thing: the last of the human freedoms—to choose one's attitude in any given set of circumstances, to choose one's own way."[2] You can choose the attitude you bring into each day and the attitude you embrace for your life.

We all get to define what will give meaning to our lives. Even for those who live in the worst of conditions, you can choose your way. In good times or bad, we can find meaning through moments of purpose. We can enrich our lives when we help give wings to someone else's dreams. And in every circumstance, we have the freedom to choose the perspective with which we will see the world.

I still lose my way, choosing to focus on what's wrong with the world instead of choosing to see my many blessings. I still lose perspective and get caught up in minutiae of the moment. I spend more time than I'd like dwelling on frustrations and annoyances I'll forget all about in a few days. That's life. But every day I get to choose how I will respond to the circumstances of my life. I get to choose how miserable I will be, or how happy. I get to choose whether I pursue the life I want to live, or let the day pass without purpose.

Whatever your starting point, you can improve your life and make it better than it is right now. Forget about perfection and appreciate any progress you make. You get to choose if you will dream big about the life you want. You get to choose whether you will find your purpose. You get to choose the life you live. Take responsibility for where you are, and get started creating the life you've imagined.

31

SEIZE THE DAY

Dead Poets Society is a thoughtful and inspiring movie about a teacher and the unorthodox way he teaches his students about literature, poetry, and life. Robin Williams plays the part of Professor Keating, a man committed to far more than the curriculum. He desires to help his students learn to think for themselves and not miss the grand adventure that everyone's life should be.

In one poignant scene, screenwriter Tom Schulman touches a theme reminiscent of Mary Oliver's evocative question, "Tell me, what is it you plan to do with your one wild and precious life?"

Professor Keating walks with his students through the halls of the school. He turns toward the trophy cases, filled with trophies, footballs, and team pictures.

Keating: Now I would like you to step forward over here and peruse some of the faces from the past.

You've walked past them many times. I don't think you've really looked at them."

The students slowly gather 'round the cases and Keating moves behind them.

Keating: They're not that different from you, are they? Same haircuts. Full of hormones, just like you. Invincible, just like you feel. The world is their oyster. They believe they're destined for great things, just like many of you. Their eyes are full of hope, just like you. Did they wait until it was too late to make from their lives even one iota of what they were capable? Because you see, gentlemen, these boys are now fertilizing daffodils. But if you listen real close, you can hear them whisper their legacy to you. Go on, lean in.

The boys lean in, and Keating hovers over their shoulders.

Keating (*whispering in a gruff voice*): Listen. You hear it? (*Whispering again.*) "Carpe. Carpe. Carpe diem. Seize the day, boys, make your lives extraordinary."[1]

How many people have gone before us? How many made their lives ones we'd want to live? Navy Seal David Goggins in his book *Can't Hurt Me* writes, "From the time you take your first breath, you become eligible to die. You also become eligible to find your greatness."[2] Life is fleeting. Don't settle for anything less than the greatness that's possible, a life that is extraordinary.

Life will end for all of us. The key is to make sure you lived a remarkable one before it does. Don't let another day go by without taking at least one step toward the life you want to live. Don't squander the chance to make your life all that it could be. Your time is now, before you are fertilizing daffodils. Seize the day. Make your life extraordinary.

32

DON'T LET UGLY STOP YOU

Despite our best efforts and diligent pursuit of purposeful moments, we will have some ugly days on the journey. How do you weather the difficult days? Take a lesson from Mike Yurosek.

Mike was a carrot farmer, and he knew all about ugly. In the 1980s, the supermarkets were very particular about the carrots they would buy from local farmers. The supermarkets knew that customers wanted carrots to be a certain size, shape, and hue of orange or they wouldn't buy them. Ugly carrots ended up rotting on the shelves. Mike found that he was throwing away as much as four hundred tons of carrots every day because they were too ugly to sell.

If ugly was the problem creating so much waste, Mike figured he could solve the problem by making his carrots less ugly. He experimented with a green bean cutter and industrial potato peeler, whittling away the unattractive parts of his twisted and misshapen carrots. The result was a small, peeled carrot that came to be known as baby carrots.[1] He launched his baby carrots in 1986, and it transformed the industry. Carrot consumption grew by almost 30 percent, and the baby carrot soon accounted for almost 70 percent of carrot sales.[2]

When life gets ugly, think about Mike's approach with his ugly carrots. How can you approach the problem from a fresh point of view? What can you strip away or peel off to make your life more enjoyable? Mike found he didn't need more, he needed less. He needed different. He got rid of the ugly parts.

What are the ugly parts of your life that keep you from living the life you want to live? Do you have habits that need trimming? Are there people who are bringing you down? Peel away all that hinders you from living the life you want, anything preventing you from living the life you've imagined. Don't allow your days to go to waste. Don't let the ugly parts of life prevent you from living the beautiful life you were meant to live.

33

THERE'S STILL TIME

L es Brown once said, "You are never too old to set another goal or to dream a new dream." If there was ever a doubt, one need only meet Nola Ochs and Yuichiro Miura. Both are an inspiration and a reminder it's never too late to pursue your dreams.

Pomp and Circumstance

Nola Ochs was born in Kansas on November 22, 1911. She grew up on the family farm and rode a horse and buggy to the one-room schoolhouse where she attended class. After high school, she began taking courses at Fort Hays State University in Kansas. That was 1930. Then Nola met Vernon Ochs. They fell in love and got married. Soon college gave way to starting a family and life on the farm.

Nola and Vernon worked the farm while raising four sons, who would give them thirteen grandchildren and fifteen great-grandchildren. But in 1972, Vernon died. Nola was sixty-one years old. She considered the possibilities of what she would do with the rest of her life. That's when going back to school first crossed her mind. Six years later, at sixty-seven, Nola Ochs returned to school at Dodge City Community College.

Over the next ten years Nola continued taking classes. It wasn't until one of her professors mentioned that she was only a few credits shy of her associate degree that Nola thought about graduating. Attending classes had been something to occupy her time. But with the possibility of an associate degree in sight, Nola decided she wanted to graduate. She finished her last few credits and received her associate degree from Dodge City Community College. She was seventy-seven years old, and she decided she wanted more.[1]

Fifty-eight years after she first began, Nola returned to Fort Hays State University to continue working toward her bachelor's degree. She left the farm and moved into student housing on campus. In 2007, ninety-five-year-old Nola Ochs graduated with her bachelor's degree, and she got to share the stage with her granddaughter Alexandra, who was also graduating.[2] But Nola wanted more. She continued her education, receiving her master's degree when she was ninety-eight, making her the oldest person in the world to complete a master's degree.

Sometimes we convince ourselves that our best days are behind us. Nola Ochs reminds us it's never too late to pursue the life we want. It took her seventy-seven years to complete a four-year college degree, but she did it! What have you left unfinished? Are you telling yourself that it's too late? Just think about Nola moving into student housing with a bunch of eighteen-year-olds when she was in her nineties. It's never too late.

Standing on Top of the World

Yuichiro Miura knows what it means to keep going, despite the difficulties. Miura was a competitive skier growing up. He made headlines when he became the first and only person to ski down Mount Everest. He was thirty-seven years old.

After this daring feat, Miura started living an unhealthy lifestyle. He took his health for granted, eating and drinking too much. By the time he was in his sixties, Miura was out of shape and in poor health. He had diabetes and heart and kidney disease. It inspired Miura to see his ninety-nine-year-old father still skiing, and it challenged him to live a better life than he was living.

Yuichiro began eating a healthy diet. He walked eleven miles a day with weights on his legs to build up stamina. And he decided he wanted to do something big. He returned to the mountain he skied down thirty years earlier. But this time he would climb it. Yuichiro wanted to become the oldest person ever to reach the summit of Mount Everest. When he was seventy years old, he accomplished his goal. And he wanted to do it again.

Three years later, Yuichiro started having cardiac arrhythmia. At seventy-three, he had heart surgery to address the issue. A year later he needed a second surgery. Despite his health issues, Miura returned to Everest and climbed to the summit a second time. He was seventy-five years old. Despite the amazing accomplishment, he was no longer the oldest person to reach the summit. The day before Yuichiro reached the summit, seventy-six-year-old Min Bahadur Sherchan stood atop the world's highest peak to capture the title of the oldest person to summit Everest. But Yuichiro Miura wasn't through yet.

Despite his health issues, Yuichiro continued his healthy diet and exercise regimen, intent on regaining his title. At seventy-six, the determined adventurer was skiing when he suffered a devastating accident. He broke his pelvis and fractured his thigh. Doctors cautioned he might never walk normally again. He exercised his way back to health and resumed his preparation to climb.

In a warm-up run to Everest, the seventy-nine-year-old Yuichiro was climbing at altitude when he suffered another cardiac episode. He left the mountain and returned to Japan for another heart surgery. While recovering from surgery, he contracted the flu. His heart stopped twice because his body was so frail.

Now eighty, having survived four heart surgeries, kidney disease, diabetes, and a fractured pelvis, Yuichiro Miura remained focused on achieving his goal of another trip to the summit of Everest. Three months after his fourth heart surgery, he returned to the Himalayas. On May 16, Yuichiro began the trek up the treacherous southwest side of the mountain. Seven days later, on May 23, Yuichiro Miura stood atop the highest mountain in the world for the third time. Once again, he regained his title as the oldest person ever to reach the summit of Mount Everest.[3]

Most eighty-year-olds struggle to walk from the house to the car. It's almost unfathomable to think about an eighty-year-old climbing the world's most challenging peak. But he had clarity on what he wanted to accomplish, and it drove him to do what was necessary to make it happen. Do you have a dream still living inside you? When are you planning on doing something about it?

The reality of your life is that today is the start of the rest of your life. You need a goal, one that will energize you to pursue, despite the obstacles that get in your way. What will it be? The life you want to live is still out there waiting for you to show up and live it. Don't stop *until* you claim the title you've been chasing. Yuichiro has already said he wants to climb Mount Everest one more time, on his ninetieth birthday. What do you want to do? Be the person you want to be. Live the life you've always imagined. It's not too late.

34

IT WILL ALL WORK OUT

One of the hardest things to do is to not make a judgment on whether the events in life are good or bad. We know how we want things to work out, and any other outcome is disappointing, if not devastating. We want the people we love to love us back. We want the company to make us an offer after the interview. But more often than we'd like, we don't get what we want, and it feels like it's derailing our plans for living the lives we dreamed of living. We aren't that good at knowing what's best, and often, we are fortunate that circumstances didn't work out like we hoped they would.

There is an old fable that captures this sentiment so well. There was a farmer who lived in a village on the outskirts of town. One morning he went out to plow his fields and found that the gate of his stables was open and his only horse was missing. The neighbor noticed the empty stable and commented, "What terrible luck that your horse has run away. How will you farm your fields?" The farmer replied, "It could be good, could be bad, who knows. But I'm sure it will all work out."

Later that afternoon the farmer was mending his fence, and he noticed a thundering rumble growing louder and louder. He looked up to see his horse charging toward the open pen, followed by a team of wild horses. In a matter of minutes there were a dozen horses secured inside the yard. The neighbor couldn't believe his eyes and exclaimed, "How lucky you are! Yesterday you had only one horse and now you have a dozen." The farmer looked at the horses and replied, "It could be good, could be bad, who knows. But I'm sure it will all work out."

The next day the farmer's son decided he would tame one of the wild stallions. He worked with the horse all day, and when he mounted the horse to ride, the horse bucked hard, throwing him to the ground, breaking his arm and leg. The neighbor saw what happened and said to the farmer, "What terrible luck. Now your son won't be able to help with the harvest." The farmer tended to his son's injuries and replied, "It could be good, could be bad, who knows. But I'm sure it will all work out."

A few days later the army rolled through town preparing for battle. They conscripted every able-bodied man to serve the king. Because the farmer's son had a broken leg and arm, they left him behind. Was it fortunate? It could be good, could be bad, who knows. But it will all work out.

Like the neighbor, we assess events as they happen, making judgments on whether they are positive or negative. But life is too complex, and it's difficult to interpret as it's happening. We need the perspective that comes with time to understand the long-term implications of the events we are living. So often the very events that disappointed us turn out to be unexpected blessings that never would have happened had it not been for the bad luck we experienced earlier.

Microsoft, Take Two

Twelve years ago I was working for a technology company called Tellme Networks. Microsoft acquired Tellme. I worked hard, and very long hours, to get the acquisition done. I felt it would be worth the effort since I would get to work for a successful and respected company like Microsoft. After many grueling months, the acquisition was complete and Tellme was part of Microsoft. Then they informed me I was being laid off.

I was disappointed, angry, and anxious about the future. I worked hard on the Tellme acquisition for the prospect of a bright future at Microsoft. In that moment, it didn't feel like things were falling into place but falling apart. There was no question in my mind, this was not good news.

I left Microsoft and joined VMware, a global leader in cloud computing. I worked at VMware for the next five years. I had five different jobs, gained fantastic professional experience in a fast-growing company, and advanced my career. I also met Vicky, who would later become my wife.

I left VMware to join a growing company called LinkedIn. I've been there almost seven years now, and the company is incredible. I love my job, I've continued to advance my career, and like the farmer in the story said, it all works out.

Three years ago Microsoft acquired LinkedIn. Microsoft is now the most valuable company in the world, and this time I got to keep my job. I know if I had stayed with Microsoft twelve years ago, I wouldn't have the incredible job I have today. And I never would have met my wonderful wife, Vicky.

Looking back, I'm grateful I got laid off twelve years ago. What I thought was terrible news at the time turned out to be a huge blessing a decade later. My life would be in a far different place had I never joined VMware. It all worked out for the better, but I needed the perspective of time for me to realize that what I thought was bad news twelve years ago was in fact fantastic news. I just didn't know it yet.

When life feels like it's falling apart, I try to remember that I'm not that good at knowing what will work out well and what won't. I try to remind myself that it all works out. Maybe not how I imagined it, but it works out.

How about you? Are there times in your life when something happened that you thought was terrible, but then ended up working out better in the long run? I'm sure it's happened to you. If you haven't taken the time to reflect on this, do. Without question, life will have times when it won't work out like you want it to. That's the time to remember: It could be good, could be bad, who knows. But I'm sure it will all work out.

35

WHAT IF IT'S TRUE?

G rowing up Irish meant growing up Catholic. Mass every Sunday and plenty of days besides. Baptism, confession, catechism, First Communion, Confirmation. When I was ten, I made an altar out of cardboard boxes and put it in my closet. Children's Bible, candles. It was like a tiny confessional booth located conveniently in my bedroom. I thought I might be a priest someday, so I figured I would get a head start.

The altar didn't last long. My mom made me take it out when she realized I was burning candles in my closet and was likely to burn down the house if my clothes caught on fire. Still, God was very real to me when I was a kid, with or without my private altar in the closet.

At some point, faith and beliefs about God have to move from what you were taught to what you believe, or don't. While I went to church my entire life, God still seemed a distant concept. I wasn't sure how religion or God applied to my everyday life, other than understanding the list of stuff I wasn't supposed to do. Some people drift away from God, the church, or religion as they grow up. Some run away. For me, I got more curious and started asking questions.

One Saturday when I was in high school, I ended up playing ultimate Frisbee with a bunch of people. I found out afterward it was a group from Young Life. I didn't know what Young Life was, but I had a lot of fun. One of my classmates invited me to come to a meeting at her house on Thursday night, so I went.

There were over one hundred high school kids crammed into the living room, spilling into the hallway and kitchen. It was a raucous and lively experience. There were seven or eight adult leaders who led the meeting. We sang songs. Not like campfire singing, more like obnoxious wailing, with lots of interaction. Kind of like a mini mosh pit with everyone sitting down and no one getting hurt.

The leaders did comedic sketches, led fun games, and held competitions. I remember they picked six people from the audience for an activity they called Chubby Bunny, a friendly competition where each person has to stuff giant marshmallows into their mouth and intelligibly say "chubby bunny." The participant who can squish the most of those puffy sugar blobs in their mouth and still say "chubby bunny" is declared the winner.

After forty-five minutes of fun, a leader named Darrell got up and talked about God. It was unlike any sermon I'd ever heard. By this time in my life I'd heard almost 1,000 sermons at church, but the way Darrell talked about God was different. It was more relatable.

It wasn't a hell, fire, and brimstone sermon. He shared stories about Jesus from the New Testament. Stories of Jesus healing a blind man he met on the road, healing a woman who had been sick and bleeding for years, calming the stormy seas. He told us about a God who created us and loves us, one who designed life and knows how to live it to the fullest. Then he asked, *What if it's true?*

I kept going to Young Life every week. I had loads of fun, and I heard more about God. I continued to ask myself, *What if it's true?* It seemed logical to me that if God created the world and everything in it, people included, that he would have some perspective on how to get the most out of it.

I studied the Bible and researched a variety of religions and philosophies. I realized that deciding how God fit into life was perhaps the most important question I could answer. A life with God would differ greatly from a life without. This was the beginning of my journey, moving from what I was taught about God as a kid to deciding what I believed about God for myself.

After reading volumes and considering the possibilities, I concluded that life made more sense with God in it, and he has been central to my life ever since. Not that it's always been easy. Forgiveness, patience, loving people who aren't that lovable? It's hard. But despite the difficulties, the facts about God and the rationale I had for believing never changed. I realized a challenging life with God is a better life than an easy one without him. I took God at his promise that life with him would be life to the fullest. I still believe that's true.

It's been decades now and life has been an adventure. Sometimes God felt close, other times distant. Sometimes I felt a great peace knowing God was in control, and sometimes I felt God was a million miles away. I've felt comfort and closeness, and I've experienced dark nights of the soul where I wrestled and screamed at God, searching for answers. I still come back to the same conclusion: to live without God would be to miss the best that life can be.

You can create an impressive life story and find happiness and adventure without God. You can find meaning and purpose, and experience joy and love. But to live your best life, life to the fullest, I think God has to be in the mix. God created you and has a plan for your life that is better than anything you can create without him.

Very Different Points of View

Blaise Pascal was a mathematician, physicist, and theologian. In his book, *Pensées*, he writes about man's craving for true happiness, and the emptiness that persists despite our efforts to fill it. He reasons the emptiness cannot be filled "since this infinite abyss can be filled only with an infinite and immutable object; in other words by God himself."[1] God created us with a place for himself in our lives. And just as a parent desires to be an integral part of their children's lives, so too does God desire to be integral to ours.

Bertrand Russell was a mathematician, philosopher, and atheist. In his autobiography he said, "The center of me is always and eternally a terrible pain, a curious wild pain, a searching for something beyond what the world contains."[2] Pascal and Russell both speak of a deep and ever-present dissatisfaction with life. Pascal concluded that only God could satisfy it, while Russell determined there was nothing in the world that ultimately would.

Pascal and Russell came to their own conclusions about

God. One believed that God created life and the other that God didn't exist. What do you think? Everyone gets to choose what they will or won't believe about God. Whether he exists, and if so, whether he's good or evil. But if there is a God who created and designed life, it's worth considering the possibilities and implications.

If God is real, and he created us with a place in our lives for him, it affects every aspect of life. Deciding what you do with God is an important enough decision that it would make sense for it to be one that is well informed.

So many people have done so many stupid things in the name of religion that many want nothing to do with God. I would encourage you to do your own study and make up your own mind. The one question to consider—*What if it's true?* What if there is a God that created life, created you, and wants you to live life to the fullest? The implications are life changing. Taking the time to explore the possibilities could be the single greatest factor in shaping the life you live.

If you want life to the fullest, don't neglect to at least consider how God may play a part in the journey. In chapter 10 of the Gospel of John, Jesus says, "I have come that they may have life, and have it to the full."[3] Isn't that what we all want, to live life to the very fullest?

Recommended Books

I've found several books particularly helpful in learning about God. If you are curious and looking for a place to start, I would recommend the following books:

Mere Christianity by C. S. Lewis. Lewis was a scholar

and a determined atheist. He couldn't reconcile that there was a loving God when there was so much evil and so much suffering in the world. Lewis's journey to Christianity included years of intellectual struggle, and he only admitted to God's existence after being convinced that faith in God was more reasonable than denying God's existence. Upon reaching that conclusion Lewis said he was "the most dejected and reluctant convert in all England." Lewis shares his logic and rationale for believing in God in his book *Mere Christianity*.

Love Does and *Everybody Always* by Bob Goff. If you struggle to consider God because of all the religious stuff, these books provide a refreshing perspective. Bob found that all too often there was so much religiousness surrounding God that it was hard to get a sense of what God was like. Bob took a very simple approach. The Bible says that God wants us to love people. Bob puts his energy into loving the people he meets while living his life. His books share his amazing journey with God and what he's learning while trying to love everybody always.

God Came Near and *Six Hours One Friday*, both by Max Lucado. Max has a gift of bringing stories to life, injecting a fresh perspective into the familiar. In *God Came Near*, Max writes about the most important moment in history . . . when God came near. And in *Six Hours One Friday*, Max looks at the last hours of Jesus's life on a cross and what it means to us.

The Shack by William P. Young. This fictional story will challenge everything you think you know about God. Thought-provoking and perspective-lending.

A Million Miles in a Thousand Years by Donald Miller. This memoir is one of my favorite books. Miller authentically shares his journey as he explores how to make his life a better story.

The Bible. If you want to find out more about God, this is the best place to start. There is a reason it's the most sold, most banned, most read, and most burned book in history. It's God's story. I would recommend you choose the New International Version and begin with the New Testament. The Gospel of Mark is a fine place to start. There are thousands of books written on the Bible, its reliability and history, and commentaries to help you understand it. Those are useful and interesting, but I found it more helpful to read the Bible itself.

36

THIS IS ALL WE CAN DO

The B-17 Flying Fortress was the workhorse of the US Air Force during WWII. They called it the Flying Fortress because it was well armed with machine guns and had heavy defensive armor so it could defend itself without needing escort fighter planes. It was such a sturdy plane that even when severely damaged in battle, they could often stay in flight long enough to get the crew back to the base safely.

In his book *The Fall of Fortresses*, Elmer Bendiner recounts his experience as a navigator aboard a B-17 Flying Fortress named the *Tondelayo*. The crew of the *Tondelayo* were on a bombing run over Germany when they came under heavy fire from German antiaircraft guns on the ground. Antiaircraft guns fire a 20 millimeter round, a devastating and powerful munition that measures six inches. The *Tondelayo* did not fare well. Many rounds hit the plane, but the crew kept it in the air and made it back to base. When the crew exited the aircraft, they saw where the shrapnel had ripped through the plane. It shocked them to see holes in the gas tanks because a

20-millimeter shell to the gas tank would typically cause the plane to explode. Luck had been on their side.

The next morning the pilot of the *Tondelayo*, Bohn Fawkes, went to look at the plane to see the damage up close. He spoke to the crew chief who was fixing the plane and commented on how lucky the crew had been that the plane hadn't exploded. The crew chief explained that it was a miracle because the gas tanks had been hit eleven times. More unbelievable was that all eleven rounds removed from the gas tanks were unexploded. One round was enough to explode the plane, and the *Tondelayo's* tanks were hit eleven times.

The crew chief wanted to know why the rounds hadn't exploded, so he sent the eleven shells to be defused, hoping he might learn more. They soon learned everything they needed to know. There wasn't a trace of explosive charge in any of the unexploded rounds. They were nothing but hollow, empty shells, except for one. One shell had a small, handwritten note tucked inside. The note read, *This is all we can do for you now.* By this time in the war, the Germans were using Jewish prisoners in their munitions factories, and even in their desperate condition they were still looking for ways to help defeat the Nazis. So rather than filling the 20-millimeter rounds with an explosive charge, they left them empty.[1]

Sometimes we see the obstacles we face, and all that we need to do, and it feels insurmountable. You want to live a life with no regrets. You want a life of meaning and purpose, but it all feels beyond your reach. John Wooden, the legendary men's basketball coach at UCLA, said, "Do not let what you cannot do interfere with what you can do." If you want to live a remarkable life, then do what you can with what you have. The prisoners couldn't do much, but what they did made an enormous difference. Their actions saved the lives of the *Tondelayo* crew. Do whatever you can, small as it may be, and the life you save may be your own.

37

MARATHON OF HOPE

I 'd say Terry Fox is the epitome of the all-American boy, but he's Canadian. Born and raised in Winnipeg, Terry was an active, athletic kid who loved to play soccer, rugby, and basketball. He exemplified determination and competitiveness, traits that would help him make a tremendous impact on millions of people around the world.

When Terry was eighteen, he started experiencing pain in his right knee. He'd been in a car accident a few months earlier and his knee had been bothering him off and on since, but it was getting worse. He had his knee examined at the hospital and found out the pain had nothing to do with the car accident. Doctors diagnosed Terry with bone cancer in his knee, and four days later, they amputated his leg. So began a journey that would touch a nation and millions of others around the world.

The night before his surgery, Terry's basketball coach, Terri Fleming, stopped by the hospital to visit. Coach Fleming gave Terry a copy of *Runner's World* magazine that contained an article on Dick Traum. Traum had his right leg amputated when he was twenty-four years old and became the first person with a prosthetic leg to complete the 26.2-mile New York City Marathon. Coach Fleming wanted to encourage Terry to see that his life wasn't over because he was having his leg amputated. Terry said thanks and set the magazine aside. Little did Fleming know that his small gift would inspire Terry Fox to run distances far greater than 26.2 miles.[1]

Fox read the article about the thirty-six-year-old Traum completing the 26.2-mile race and believed that if Traum could run a marathon, then he could run a marathon every day. Fox would later write, "It was then I decided to meet this new challenge head on and not only overcome my disability, but conquer it in such a way that I could never look back and say it disabled me."[2] Terry Fox's idea for the Marathon of Hope was born. But it would have to wait. First, he needed to undergo the operation to remove his right leg and then endure months of chemotherapy.

Terry went through sixteen months of chemotherapy and physiotherapy. While the chemo treatments were grueling, Terry knew that he wasn't the only one battling for his life. Others, including small children, surrounded him, enduring the same agony he was. Some were facing the challenge with a brave face, while despair and hopelessness consumed others. Terry was optimistic that he would overcome his cancer, but he knew that most people he met at the cancer center wouldn't. He didn't want to leave knowing that all those he left behind were still suffering. Cancer needed a cure for the hurting to stop. He would give everything he had for that cause.

Fox decided he would run across Canada, 5,300 miles, to

raise awareness and money for cancer research. And he would do it one marathon at a time, running 26 miles every day. Terry was ready to put his plan in motion, and he started by sharing his vision with his best friend, Doug Alward.

The idea shocked Doug since he knew that Terry never enjoyed running even when he had two legs. But he did what best friends do—he told Terry he was with him no matter what. Terry and Doug started training. At first, Terry couldn't even run a quarter of a mile. He had to run with a strange hop-and-skip-type motion, and he often fell as he learned to run with a prosthetic leg. But Doug could see Terry's determination. Doug noted, "He seemed to have a sense of destiny that this was his mission. I guess being in the children's ward with kids dying of cancer right in front of him, he said, 'I gotta do something about this.'"[3]

After months of training, it was time to begin. Terry would run from the Atlantic Ocean to the Pacific, across Canada, with a goal of raising $1 million along the way. He called it the Marathon of Hope. In a donated van, Terry and Doug hit the road. The first stop was St. John's, Newfoundland. On April 12, 1980, Terry stepped into the Atlantic Ocean, where he filled two bottles with water, one that he would keep as a souvenir and the other he would pour into the Pacific Ocean at the end of the journey. The Marathon of Hope had begun.

It was a rough start. Terry faced wind and rain and snow, but it was more discouraging for him that few people came out to support what he was doing. At the beginning, the Marathon of Hope was not receiving a lot of attention. But Isadore Sharp noticed.

Sharp was the founder and CEO of the Four Seasons

Hotels. He noticed what Terry was doing, and he called him. "I spoke with Terry one day from a pay phone when he was in the East Coast. I could sense despair in his voice and suggested a plan. I would pledge $2 for every mile Terry ran and would challenge companies across the country to do the same. We created an ad in the newspapers that read 'Let's make Terry's Run count.' If we could get a thousand companies to participate, we could raise $10 million for cancer research. Terry's mood changed and he said that's all I need." For Sharp this was about more than encouraging a courageous kid running across Canada. It was personal. Sharp's eighteen-year-old son died of cancer two years earlier, around the same time that Terry was first diagnosed.[4]

Isadore Sharp's support encouraged Terry. Crowds were getting bigger, and more people were paying attention. Terry began dreaming bigger. He figured if every Canadian would give just $1, they would raise $23 million for cancer research. That became his new goal.

Soon newspapers and news reports were tracking Terry's progress in the Marathon of Hope. He was capturing the hearts of a nation and inspiring people of Canada and the world. One of those Terry inspired was Rick Hansen.

Rick suffered a spinal cord injury when he was fifteen years old. He was in the back of a pickup truck and thrown out of the moving vehicle. The accident left him a paraplegic. The Marathon of Hope inspired Rick to raise awareness and money for spinal cord injury research. If Terry could make a difference by running across Canada for cancer, then Rick could make a difference by wheeling himself in his wheelchair around the world for spinal cord injuries.

Rick Hansen would later spend twenty-six months on his

Man in Motion tour. He wheeled himself through thirty-four countries covering 24,890 miles, averaging 70 miles a day. He raised awareness of the potential of people with disabilities and raised $26 million to fund spinal cord injury research.[5] Terry's Marathon of Hope was having an impact in ways he never imagined. It's a wonderful reminder that we never know the full impact of our actions. Any act of courage or kindness has the potential to make a significant impact beyond anything you thought possible.

Four months into the Marathon of Hope, Terry was struggling. The constant running left him exhausted, having chest pains and suffering regular coughing fits. He went to see a doctor and received the news that his cancer had returned, only this time it was in his lungs. On September 1, after running 3,339 miles in 143 days, Terry Fox ended his Marathon of Hope so he could begin cancer treatment.[6]

Over the coming months, Terry received truckloads of mail. People from across the world, including Pope John Paul II, sent letters of support and encouragement. Fox received many awards, including the Companion of the Order of Canada, the highest level of the Order of Canada, awarded to those who have shown the highest merit to Canada and humanity. He was the youngest recipient ever to receive the honor. And while Terry's run stopped on September 1, donations to the Marathon of Hope continued, surpassing Terry's goal of $23 million.

For Terry, the marathon was never about him; it was about finding a cure, helping the many people suffering with cancer. He said, "Even if I don't finish, we need others to continue. It's got to keep going without me."[7] Terry Fox died on June 28, 1981. He was twenty-two years old. But his legacy and impact would continue.

On September 13, 1981, Isadore Sharp and Terry's family organized the Terry Fox Run. It was a tribute to Terry and would continue his efforts to raise money for cancer research, just as Terry had hoped. Over 300,000 people took part in the event. It raised $3.5 million for cancer research.[8]

And the event was just the beginning. The Terry Fox Run has become an annual event across Canada and the world. Over sixty countries have hosted a Terry Fox Run, and each year over three million people take part. To date, the Terry Fox Run has raised more than $750 million for cancer research.[9] And in an interesting turn of events, Dick Traum was so inspired by the event he founded the Achilles Track Club, an organization dedicated to encouraging people with disabilities to take part in mainstream athletics. It provides support and training for people with all kinds of disabilities, including visual impairment, cerebral palsy, amputation, multiple sclerosis, and people in wheelchairs, with crutches, and with prostheses. The Achilles Track Club, later renamed Achilles International, is now in seventy countries and is the largest of its kind.[10] Another example of the extended influence of Terry's actions.

Terry Fox set out to help people suffering with cancer. He set an audacious goal of running across Canada to raise awareness and money for cancer research. Today treatments exist because of the research funded by Terry's Marathon of Hope and the Terry Fox Run.[11] People are alive today because a twenty-two-year-old saw beyond himself and wanted to make things better for others. And he did something about it. He dreamed big and took bold action.

There's so much we can take from Terry's story. He had determination like Teddy Roosevelt. He had a single-minded purpose like Andrew Carnegie. Terry found a purpose that was bigger than himself. It was personal. He knew what it was like to suffer with cancer, and he remembered the faces of those he left behind in the cancer ward. Terry gave wings to their dreams just as others helped give wings to Terry's.

His best friend, Doug, stepped up and traveled every mile with Terry. Isadore Sharp gave Terry financial support and rallied the support of other businesses. The cheering crowds gave wings to Terry, boosting his morale and energy so he could carry on despite the blisters and fatigue. Participants in the annual Terry Fox Run keep Terry's dream alive. And the millions of people who donated to the Marathon of Hope and the Terry Fox Run gave wings to his dream of finding a cure for cancer.

Terry's influence is now reaching a new generation of kids inspired by his Marathon of Hope. In 2019, a seven-year-old boy named Ethan Smallwood dressed up as his hero, Terry Fox, for Halloween. He donned a curly-haired wig to match Terry's distinctive 1980s hairstyle. He sported the same gray shorts and white T-shirt with "Marathon of Hope" written across the front, the same shirt that Terry wore every day of his run. Ethan wore a stocking to emulate Terry's prosthetic leg. And Ethan raised money to help with cancer research like Terry did.

Instead of asking for Halloween candy, Ethan asked people for donations to further cancer research. Thirty-eight years after Terry Fox ended his Marathon of Hope, Ethan continued the effort, raising another $16,000 for the cause.[12]

What Terry started is still going. And as long as there are people like Ethan Smallwood, it will continue.

Terry found perspective during his struggle with cancer. He found the silver lining of his struggle. He said, "I guess that one of the most important things I've learned is that nothing is ever completely bad. Even cancer. It has made me a better person. It has given me courage and a sense of purpose I never had before. But you don't have to do like I did . . . wait until you lose a leg or get some awful disease, before you take the time to find out what kind of stuff you're really made of. You can start now. Anybody can." [13] Are you struggling with difficulties? Keep searching for the positives hidden in the experience. Problems bring possibilities.

No matter what your situation is, you can make a difference. Take hope from the life of a curly-headed twenty-two-year-old who had the courage to dream big and take action. What's your dream? What purpose will you pursue? Imagine the possibilities. Find your purpose and take action. Your life can accomplish more than you ever imagined.

WILL THIS WORK?

E leven years, ten months, and two days ago, I was one day away from dying. Then I received an organ transplant that saved my life. I could now finish living my life. I had the chance to live it better than before. When I first woke up after surgery, appreciation for a second chance at life wasn't top of mind for me. I was too busy trying to figure out what happened to me.

I don't remember being aware of anything. I couldn't see or feel, there wasn't a thought in my mind. Someone spoke into the darkness, *You are at Stanford Hospital, you've had a liver transplant, and I will remove the tube from your throat.* None of that made any sense. The last thing I remember was being at Good Samaritan Hospital for observation after my gall-bladder surgery. *Stanford? Transplant?* I thought I was one of those medical mix-up stories where doctors perform the wrong surgery on a patient.

Faces slowly came into focus. With the tube removed from my throat, I could speak. *What happened?* A doctor filled me in. I had been in a coma; I had come very close to dying, and I was fortunate to have received a liver transplant that saved my life. This left me with more questions than answers.

I had tubes coming out of my body in several places. I found notes written across my chest in permanent marker saying I had a pacemaker. I had a beard for the first time in my life because I hadn't shaved while in the coma. Because I knew little about what happened, and nothing about transplants, I inundated my doctors and nurses with a barrage of questions, followed by more questions.

They had me hooked up to a plethora of machines. A cacophony of beeps and noises echoed through the room. They gave me handfuls of pills, and as many injections. I wanted to know what each was and what it did. Not knowing anything about transplants, I didn't understand what was happening. I remember asking a nurse when I could stop taking all this medication, and she told me to get used to it because I would need to take pills for the rest of my life if I wanted to stay alive.

With the anesthesia out of my system, I started feeling a lot of pain. During the twelve hours of surgery doctors had opened my chest and unpacked all my organs so they could swap out my liver for the healthy, donated one, then stitched and stapled me back together, inside and out. I lost 40 pounds in the previous two weeks, leaving me rail thin. At six three, I weighed less than 160 pounds. I had never felt so weak or hopeless in my life.

Two days later, a nurse came to my room and told me it was time to go to a support group. She helped me into a wheelchair, and we headed for the meeting. I thought I would join the other transplant patients, and I'd be able to get my questions answered. I was mistaken.

When I wheeled into the room, there were about thirty-five or forty people already there. I was the only one in a wheelchair and the only person wearing a hospital gown. It looked like I was the last to arrive because we got started right away. A hospital volunteer welcomed everyone and suggested that we go around the room and introduce ourselves. They started on the opposite side of the room, so I sat back and listened. I realized this was not what I was expecting.

The first person to speak was a man in his fifties. He told us his name and then added that he needed a kidney. He had been on the transplant waiting list for almost four years. Next, a woman in her forties said she needed a liver transplant and had been waiting for two years. One by one, they shared how long they had been waiting for a transplant. I realized that I was in a room of people still waiting, a support group of people trying to stay hopeful while waiting for the lifesaving transplants they all needed. I was the only person in the room who had received one. I felt panicked. *What was I doing here? How would they feel when they heard I received a transplant after one day on the waiting list? Why did I get a transplant when they had all been waiting so long, some over seven years?* I just wanted to leave and get as far away from this support group as I could.

I tried to get the nurse to bring me back to my room, but she assured me it would be all right. Introductions continued, and my anxiety grew. Soon everyone else had gone, and it was my turn.

I told them my story and shared that I never knew I

needed a transplant. I was never on the waiting list. After being in a coma, I woke to find I had received a liver transplant. I paused. They cheered. It shocked me. I expected bitterness and resentment. Instead, they responded with joy and celebration. It was a profound and moving experience.

On my way back to my room I asked my nurse why they were so gracious and not angry that I had received a transplant when they didn't. She told me I reminded them that there is hope. Every story of someone having a successful transplant meant that the same could happen for them. I had a much deeper appreciation for how special a gift my transplant was.

I had a much greater appreciation for how fragile life is, and a deeper desire to make the most of my remaining days. I knew I didn't want my life to end with regrets, or live with the agony of an untold story. I would be more intentional about living my days to the fullest.

This book is about my journey and the things I've done to live a better life. It's about having a fresh perspective and appreciating what I already have. I've shared how I've learned to find meaning and purpose in places I hadn't before. My life is better, and these are the ideas and actions that worked for me. The question is, will they work for you?

Will your life be perfect? No. Will everything turn out exactly how you want it to? Of course not. Will your life be better? I think so. I know mine is.

Life is for living. There will be good days and bad. There will be messy parts no matter how hard you try to avoid them. Life involves people and people come with complications. They are messy, emotional, and imperfect. A remarkable life requires ideas and actions to overcome the complicating factors, strategies for living a life with few regrets, despite the messiness.

Luck plays its part. Some will have more of it than others. Look hard enough and you'll always find someone better off than you are, and worse. There's no guarantee of fairness in life. You get what you get. It's yours to make the most of. Hockey legend Wayne Gretzky captures it so well: "You miss 100 percent of the shots you don't take." This book is about taking the shots necessary to live your best life.

Your life won't improve just by reading a book. If you want to live a better life, do something with what you've learned. Otherwise, nothing changes. You'll end your life having lived less of it than you wanted to and less than what was possible.

Near the beginning of WWII, Winston Churchill was addressing the students of Harrow School, a boarding school for boys in London Churchill himself had attended. Those were trying times of uncertainty and fear, with war raging and the survival of British society in question. In his closing remarks, Churchill spoke passionately of the lessons learned in the war. He shared these words of encouragement with the students:

> Never give in. Never give in. Never, never, never,
> never, in nothing, great or small, large or petty, never
> give in, except to convictions of honour and good
> sense. Never yield to force. Never yield to the appar-
> ently overwhelming might of the enemy.[1]

It's a fitting sentiment on which to end. Never give in. Don't stop pursuing the life you want to live. Never give up seeking moments and opportunities of purpose. Never, never, never forget how fragile and precious your life is. Don't yield to the criticism of others, or settle for the effortless outcomes of living an unintentional life. Fight the enemies of regret and fear. Have the courage to live. Fully. In the arena, pursuing everything you have imagined your life to be. Your life is your story. Don't leave it untold. Don't leave it unlived. A remarkable life is in the living, not in the dreaming or planning. Go. Try. Do. Experience. Give. Love. Your life has already begun. Don't miss another minute.

Tell me, what is it you will now do with your one wild and precious life?

EPILOGUE

S ince my transplant, I've had the chance to do so much. Life hasn't been perfect, but I feel fortunate for the extra 4,300 days of life I've been able to live. In two months I will celebrate the twelfth anniversary of my transplant. It's been an extraordinary twelve years. These are my bonus years, the ones I almost missed. How would you spend an extra twelve years of life if they were given to you?

Forget the hypothetical—how have you spent the last twelve years of your life? Have you made the most of it? Appreciated it? Have you been intentional about watching sunsets and "I love you"s? Are you satisfied with the life you've lived?

Every year on the anniversary of my transplant I celebrate with my family. We look back on all the experiences we've been able to share because of the transplant. It's a wonderful exercise because it reminds me of all I would have missed. I would encourage you to do the same. Look back over the last decade. Write about the experiences you had, those you loved, maybe some you didn't. And make a second list of the things you wish were on your first list. Those would be the things you should get going on now.

Below are a few of the highlights I've had since my transplant, experiences I almost missed out on. I'm so grateful I didn't.

- I got to see my three kids graduate from high school.
- I brought my kids to Ireland and showed them where I lived as a kid. We walked the fields of my grandfather's land and visited the places where my mom and dad grew up. Sharing where you're from with your kids is a don't-miss experience.
- I visited the beaches of Normandy, which was at the top of my list of places I most wanted to see. The history of D-Day, the sacrifices of so many that paved the way for me to live a life in peace and freedom. It was a sobering and moving trip, and one I'm so glad I got to experience.
- Aidan loves music, so when he turned sixteen years old, I surprised him with a father-son trip to Cleveland, Ohio. Cleveland isn't a place most people would be excited to see, but it had a few things magical for Aidan. We went to the Rock & Roll Hall of Fame, where Aidan read every sign on every exhibit at least once. Most visitors spend two to three hours taking in the exhibits. We shut the place down. We were there for almost seven hours and loved every minute. Then we went to a small nightclub to see one of Aidan's favorite bands

perform. We braved the mosh pit and the crowds, and Aidan experienced a memorable live show. We went to B Spot burger joint, voted to have the Best Burgers in America, and we put it to the test. The entire trip spoke to things Aidan loves, and it was fantastic.

- When Brendan turned sixteen, he thought I was taking him to Cleveland for his birthday too, but I surprised him with a special father-son trip to Wisconsin. Brendan is a rabid Green Bay Packers fan, so there was only one possibility for his trip. Brendan and I headed to Lambeau Field, home of the Green Bay Packers. We ate at the Brett Favre Steakhouse and attended a special Packers tailgate party. We got great seats on the forty-yard line and got to see a close-up view of the Packers beating the Cleveland Browns. Of all the trips Brendan will ever take in his life, I'm not sure anything will top our trip to Lambeau.

- Kylie is sharp. She knew that she and I would be taking a father-daughter trip when she turned sixteen. She made it known that she wanted to go to Paris. I would say, "Kylie, Aidan went to Ohio and Brendan went to Wisconsin. Do you think it would be fair for you to go to France?" We went to France. And it's something every dad should do with his daughter. The Eiffel Tower, the catacombs, Versailles, the Louvre, and Musée d'Orsay. Everything was perfect, and possible only because my transplant gave me the gift of more time.

- I wanted to make sure my family had a lifetime of

memories together. Every year we embark on our Delaney Family Adventure, going somewhere we've never been, doing something we've never done. In my extra dozen years we've visited Hawaii, Disney World, the Caribbean, Boston, Cape Cod, and New York. We had Philly cheesesteaks in Philadelphia, ate hot chicken in Nashville, visited Graceland and Sun Studio in Memphis. We went to Costa Rica, London, Detroit, Chicago, Seattle, and Dallas, and we're now working our way through all fifty states. And we have a lifetime of wonderful memories, and many more trips to come.

- I got to see nieces and nephews born, married, and have children of their own.
- I experienced the pain of getting divorced, and all that comes with it. Life on borrowed time still has its difficulties, its pain, and its wonder.
- But every painful process makes new experiences possible, and one of the most incredible experiences in my life was marrying Vicky. We eloped in Central Park, New York, and it was storybook wonderful. I could write another book on the amazing parts of life I've experienced with Vicky since. It all serves to remind me it's all extra.

When I turned forty-nine years old, my kids gave me an empty photo album, along with a list of fifty things they wanted me to do before I turned fifty. The instructions said I was to take pictures doing everything on the list so I could fill the empty photo album. And thus began perhaps the most intentional year of living I've ever had.

It's fascinating to see what other people think you should do with your life, and amusing to see what my kids believed was possible to accomplish in 365 days. We're a few years past my fiftieth birthday, and I'm still not done with all fifty to-dos on the list, but I've finished a respectable thirty-five.

The kids didn't sandbag the goals either. We tried all thirty-one flavors of Baskin-Robbins ice cream (in one sitting), watched a sunrise and sunset on the same day, visited Presidential Libraries, and took cooking classes. I learned to play the saxophone and use chopsticks, read all of John Steinbeck's novels, went vegetarian for a day, and got a beautiful Rickenbacker electric guitar. We went sailing, zip-lining, and horseback riding, flew in helicopters and hot air balloons, tried caviar, and saw Ed Sheeran in concert. Number 25 on the list? Write a book, and with *A Life Worth Living*, I was able to check another one off the list.

I was to meet someone famous. Over the course of twelve months I crossed paths with radio shock jock Howard Stern, surfer and author Bethany Hamilton, George Wendt (the actor who played Norm on *Cheers*), former Speaker of the House Newt Gingrich, and Motley Crue lead singer Vince Neil. I'm still working on meeting the president of the United States, learning to speak a new language, and experiencing New Year's Eve in Times Square. I tried and failed learning to knit and read music. But what an incredible, intentional year of living it was.

The list goes on, and that's the point. Life is a collection of experiences. Our goal is to collect well. Days turn into months, which turn into years, which become your life. I hope that you find ideas in these pages that help you live the life you want to live, a life filled with purpose, one you will look back on with few regrets.

Now it's time to act. Find your purpose. Dare to live the life you've imagined. It's up to you to create the life you want to live. Don't settle for less. Make the most of every moment you have. It's never too late to change your story.

Tell me, what is it you plan to do with your one, wild and precious life?

ABOUT THE AUTHOR

Kevin John Delaney is the Vice President of Learning & Development at LinkedIn. Prior to that Kevin spent 20 years in high tech, worked for Young Life, a non-profit organization, and failed in his attempts to make a living as a musician.

In 2008, Kevin suffered a series of health issues that left him in a coma, very close to dying. He got a second chance at life when he received an organ transplant that saved his life. He lives in San Jose, California with his wife, a dozen guitars, and a baby grand piano. He has three adult children who help make his life a daring adventure.

ACKNOWLEDGMENTS

I'm reminded every day how the people and events in my life have shaped me. This book was born from all of those experiences, good and bad. I wouldn't be who I am without them, and my story wouldn't be what it is.

This book would not exist without the support and encouragement of my wife, Vicky. I am beyond lucky to have you in my life. You are my first reader, chief encourager, and biggest fan. You are an operational wonder and an extraordinary partner. I would choose you for any and every endeavor. You improve my life in a thousand ways. Thank you for helping make this book a reality.

A Life Worth Living is filled with stories of people who have inspired me, and inspiration was an important component in creating this book. Bob Goff, Maurice Cheeks, Nick Palermo, Staff Sergeant Johnny Jones, Jamie Foxx, Diana Nyad, Robert Leibowitz, Richie Sully, Yuichiro Miura, Tricia Seaman, Tony Robbins, Lois Gibson, Jordan Kinyera, James Harrison, Dave Walsh, Scott Harrison, Richard, Serena and

Venus Williams, and the anonymous organ donor who saved my life—thank you for inspiring me.

To my parents, Patrick and Dolores Delaney. You've influenced my life in profound and lasting ways. Your stories shaped mine. Thank you for the many sacrifices you made to give me the life I have. Families go through many seasons, some up and some down. I'm grateful for the season we are in. I appreciate you more every day.

I am a product of the many books I've read, and the podcasts and audio programs I've listened to. One of the most influential and impactful people on my journey has been Jim Rohn. I never met Jim, but his ideas have shaped my thinking and affected my life. Donald Miller, Bob Goff and Mitch Albom have all written words that have stirred my soul. Their books should be a part of everyone's library.

Thank you to Jess Amortegui, Carly Cohen, James Estes, Marc Prager, and Nathan Tanner for reading an early draft of this book. Your feedback and encouragement was both insightful and helpful.

To Christina Roth, my editor. Thank you for your guidance, patience, and expertise. You were a steady hand guiding me through unknown waters. The book is better because of you.

I can't imagine life without my kids, Aidan, Brendan and Kylie. You make me want to live a better life. You've added adventure and uncertainty, joy and fear. You add all the stuff that makes life wonderful. Thank you for encouraging me to write a book. I hope you find some encouragement and inspiration to live life to the fullest. My hope for you is that you create a life worth living, one filled with purpose, meaning and faith.

God has been integral in making my life all that it is. George Nowicki, Nick Palermo, Dave Walsh, Kevin Wood, Bob and Missy Scudder, Marty Caldwell, Steve Chung, Alan Smyth—you've all played a part in helping me understand God more, and making my life a better adventure.

A special thanks to James Estes. Your invitation to join you in a 100-Day Challenge was the catalyst I needed to finish writing this book. You are one of the most authentic people I know. You never stop striving to be the man you want to be. I appreciate your heart, and your unconditional friendship throughout the years.

To Vicky, while I've acknowledged you already, I can never thank you enough for all you do. You give my life more purpose; you help me dare to live the life I've imagined. You make my life worth living.

NOTES

Introduction

1. Mary Oliver, "The Summer Day," *Devotions* (New York: Penguin Press, 2017).

1. Everyone, Everywhere

1. *Home Alone*, directed by Chris Columbus, written by John Hughes (Los Angeles: Twentieth Century Fox, 1990).
2. World Health Organization, "Depression," accessed April 24, 2020, https://www.who.int/news-room/fact-sheets/detail/depression.

2. The Happiest Guy I Ever Met

1. Martin McNeil, "Ricky Berry's Suicide Still a Mystery," *LA Times*, August 19, 1990, https://www.latimes.com/archives/la-xpm-1990-08-19-sp-2909-story.html.

3. The Gift of Perspective

1. Mark Manson, "7 Strange Questions That Help You Find Your Life Purpose," Markmanson.net, March 20, 2015, https://markmanson.net/life-purpose.
2. Daewoung Kim and Youngseo Choi, "Dying for a Better Life: South Koreans Fake Their Funerals for Life Lessons," Reuters, November 5, 2019, https://www.reuters.com/article/us-southkorea-livingfunerals/dying-for-a-better-life-south-koreans-fake-their-funerals-for-life-lessons-idUSKBN1XG038.

4. How Will You Be Remembered?

1. Evan Andrews, "Did a Premature Obituary Inspire the Nobel Prize?," History.com, August 22, 2018, https://www.history.com/news/did-a-premature-obituary-inspire-the-nobel-prize.
2. "Nobel Prize Facts," Nobel Media AB 2020, August 2, 2020, https://www.nobelprize.org/prizes/facts/nobel-prize-facts/.

5. Regret

1. Steven Pressfield, *The War of Art: Break Through the Blocks and Win Your Inner Creative Battles* (New York: Black Irish Entertainment LLC, 2002).
2. Bronnie Ware, *The Top Five Regrets of the Dying: A Life Transformed by the Dearly Departing* (Carlsbad, CA: Hay House, 2011).
3. Theodore Roosevelt, "The Strenuous Life" speech, Chicago, Illinois, April 10, 1899, Voicesofdemocracy.umd.edu, https://voicesofdemocracy.umd.edu/roosevelt-strenuous-life-1899-speech-text/.

7. Dream Big

1. Cathy Free, "Special Needs Teacher Dies with a Secret Fortune — and Leaves $1 Million to Her Former School," People.com, June 22, 2018, https://people.com/human-interest/special-needs-teacher-leaves-1-million-former-school/.
2. Libby Kane, "No one realized this 92-year-old janitor had quietly amassed an $8 million fortune until they read his will," Business Insider, February 13, 2015, https://www.businessinsider.com/ronald-read-secret-millionaire-2015-2.
3. Sasha Ingber, "Social Worker Led Frugal Life To Leave Nearly $11 Million To Children's Charities," NPR.org, December 29, 2018, https://www.npr.org/2018/12/29/680883772/social-worker-led-frugal-life-to-donate-nearly-11-million-to-childrens-charities.
4. Health Resources & Services Administration, "Organ Donation Statistics," accessed May 3, 2020, https://www.organdonor.gov/statistics-stories/statistics.html.

8. Welcome to the Arena

1. Theodore Roosevelt, "Citizenship in a Republic" speech, the Sorbonne in Paris, April 23, 1910, TheodoreRooseveltCenter.org, February 19, 2015, https://www.theodorerooseveltcenter.org/Blog/Item/Man%20in%20the%20Arena.

9. Don't Settle for Less

1. David C. M. Carter, *Breakthrough: Learn the Secrets of the World's Leading Mentor and Become the Best You Can Be,* (New York, Jeremy P. Tarcher, 2012).
2. Joyce Chen, "Sylvester Stallone Reveals He Once Sold His Dog Butkus When He Was Broke, Bought Him Back for $15K," USMagazine.com, March 31, 2017, https://www.usmagazine.com/celebrity-news/news/sylvester-stallone-shares-sweet-throwback-pics-of-dog-butkus-w474367/.
3. Darren Sugiyama, *Living Outside the Cubicle: The Ultimate Success Guide for the Aspiring Entrepreneur* (self-pub., Lulu Press, 2012).
4. Chen, "Sylvester Stallone Reveals He Once Sold His Dog Butkus When He Was Broke."

11. A New Point of View

1. Mitch Albom, *Tuesdays with Morrie: An Old Man, a Young Man, and Life's Greatest Lesson* (New York: Doubleday, 2002).
2. Terence McArdle, "How the 1911 Theft of the Mona Lisa Made It the World's Most Famous Painting," *Washington Post,* October 20, 2019, https://www.washingtonpost.com/history/2019/10/20/how-theft-mona-lisa-made-it-worlds-most-famous-painting/; Sheena McKenzie, "Mona Lisa: The Theft That Created a Legend," CNN.com, November 19, 2013, https://www.cnn.com/2013/11/18/world/europe/mona-lisa-the-theft/index.html.
3. World Health Organization, "Global Data on Visual Impairment," accessed May 14, 2020, https://www.who.int/blindness/publications/globaldata/en/.
4. Helen Keller, "Three Days to See," *The Atlantic,* January 1933, https://

www.theatlantic.com/magazine/archive/1933/01/three-days-to-see/371679/.

5. Reeve Staff, "A Single Centimeter, a Ruined Life: The Accident That Caused Christopher Reeve (Superman) to Go from a Star to Legend," Christopher & Dana Reeve Foundation, June 8, 2020, https://www.christopherreeve.org/blog/daily-dose/a-single-centimeter-a-ruined-life-the-accident-that-caused-christopher-reeve-superman-to-go-from-a-star-to-legend.

6. Reeve Staff, "Prevalence of Paralysis in the United States," Christopher & Dana Reeve Foundation, accessed April 24, 2020, https://www.christopherreeve.org/living-with-paralysis/stats-about-paralysis.

7. World Bank, "Disability Inclusion," updated May 15, 2020, https://www.worldbank.org/en/topic/disability.

8. World Health Organization, "Deafness and Hearing Loss," March 1, 2020, https://www.who.int/news-room/fact-sheets/detail/deafness-and-hearing-loss.

9. Victoria Richards, "Boyfriend Proposes to Deaf Woman Hearing for First Time in Emotional Video," *Independent*, March 17, 2016, https://www.independent.co.uk/news/world/americas/deaf-woman-cochlear-implant-hearing-first-time-boyfriend-proposes-emotional-video-mississippi-a6936681.html.

10. Centers for Disease Control and Prevention, "Global WASH Fast Facts," accessed April 24, 2020, https://www.cdc.gov/healthywater/global/wash_statistics.html.

11. World Health Organization, "Drinking-Water," accessed April 24, 2020, https://www.who.int/news-room/fact-sheets/detail/drinking-water.

12. What's Not Wrong

1. "Wounded Warrior 'Joey' Jones: This Thanksgiving I'm Thankful for America—and a Superpower We All Have," FoxNews.com, November 27, 2019, https://www.foxnews.com/opinion/wounded-warrior-joey-jones-this-thanksgiving-im-thankful-for-america-you-should-be-too.

2. Patrick Filbin, "Nine Years after War Took Marine's Legs, New Causes Give Him Purpose," *Chattanooga Times Free Press* (TN), November 18, 2019, https://www.military.com/daily-news/2019/11/18/nine-years-after-war-took-marines-legs-new-causes-give-him-purpose.html.

15. Single-Minded Purpose

1. Masooma M., "Andrew Carnegie: A Tale of Struggle and Success," Samarly.com, accessed March 18, 2020, https://samarly.com/index.php/success-stories/andrew-carnegie-tale-struggle-success/.
2. Jim Rohn, *The Treasury of Quotes* (Melbourne, Australia: Brolga Publishing, 2006).
3. "Philanthropy of Andrew Carnegie," Columbia University Libraries, accessed April 25, 2020, https://library.columbia.edu/libraries/rbml/units/carnegie/andrew.html.
4. Ahmed Sule, "Richard Williams: The Tenacity of a Black Father," Operation Black Vote, July 2, 2014, https://www.obv.org.uk/news-blogs/richard-williams-tenacity-black-father.
5. Reeves Wiedeman, "Child's Play," *New Yorker*, June 2, 2014, https://www.newyorker.com/magazine/2014/06/02/childs-play-6.
6. "Venus Williams," Women's Tennis Association Stats, WTAtennis.com, accessed March 27, 2020, https://www.wtatennis.com/players/230220/venus-williams.
7. "Career Prize Money Leaders," Women's Tennis Association stats, WTAtennis.com, accessed March 27, 2020, http://wtafiles.wtatennis.com/pdf/rankings/All_Career_Prize_Money.pdf.
8. "Williams Sister Shot by Gangster Defending Crack House, Court Told," ABC News, October 25, 2004, https://www.abc.net.au/news/2004-10-26/williams-sister-shot-by-gangster-defending-crack/573876.

16. From One to Many

1. Jeff Chesemore, "Young Life Gave Me a Voice," *Relationships*, Spring 2012, https://www.younglife.org/Relationships/Pages/2012/04/YoungLifeGaveMeaVoice.aspx.

17. Moments of Purpose

1. Sara Kettler, "Robin Williams and Christopher Reeve's Devoted Friendship Began as Juilliard Roommates," Biography.com, May 20, 2020, https://www.biography.com/news/robin-williams-christopher-reeve-friendship.

2. Rebecca Lawrence, "Robin Williams' Unique Way of Helping Quadriplegic Christopher Reeves and His Guilt over John Belushi's Death Are Revealed in New Documentary," DailyMail.com, August 8, 2019, https://www.dailymail.co.uk/tvshowbiz/article-7337679/Robin-Williams-unique-way-helping-quadriplegic-Christopher-Reeves-revealed-new-documentary.html.

3. Steve Sypa, "Jackie Robinson-Pee Wee Reese Statue in Front of MCU Park Vandalized with Swastikas, Racial Epithets," Amazinavenue.com, August 8, 2013, https://www.amazinavenue.com/2013/8/8/4601796/jackie-robinson-pee-wee-reese-statue-vandalized-racism-mcu-park.

4. History.com Editors, "Jackie Robinson Breaks Color Barrier," History.com, accessed April 14, 2020, https://www.history.com/this-day-in-history/jackie-robinson-breaks-color-barrier.

5. Harold Uhlman, "Pee Wee and Jackie," LADodgerTalk.com, May 13, 2020, https://ladodgertalk.com/2020/05/13/pee-wee-and-jackie/.

6. Roger Kahn, "The Day Jackie Robinson Was Embraced," *New York Times*, April 21, 2007, https://www.nytimes.com/2007/04/21/opinion/l21robinson.html.

7. Jayshox, "Maurice Cheeks National Anthem with Natalie Gilbert," YouTube Video, 2:10, January 7, 2013, https://www.youtube.com/watch?v=Sin9M9boANo.

8. Sean Deveney, "Hall of Famer Maurice Cheeks Recalls National Anthem Assist: 'I Didn't Know I Would Do That,'" Sportingnews.com, September 7, 2018, https://www.sportingnews.com/us/nba/news/maurice-mo-cheeks-national-anthem-natalie-gilbert-video-coach-nba-hall-of-fame-trail-blazers/h749s8eomo4l1gy86ju2g9r26.

9. Darnell Mayberry, "Star-Spangled Save: What Maurice Cheeks Did for Anthem Singer in Portland Is Still Remembered," Oklahoman.com, April 13, 2010, https://oklahoman.com/article/3413717/star-spangled-save-what-maurice-cheeks-did-for-anthem-singer-in-portland-is-still-remembered.

10. Harriet Agerholm, "Bus Driver Praised for Kicking All His Passengers off Because No One Would Make Room for Wheelchair User," *Independent*, November 1, 2018, https://www.independent.co.uk/news/world/europe/bus-driver-hero-wheelchair-user-passengers-paris-france-public-transport-a8613206.html.

11. Nick Palermo, *Missing Stars, Fallen Sparrows* (Maitland, Florida: Xulon Press, 2013).

18. Give Wings to Others

1. Megan Willets, "A Generous Christmas Gift Is the Reason Harper Lee Got to Write 'To Kill a Mockingbird,'" *Business Insider*, February 19, 2016, https://www.businessinsider.com/harper-lees-present-to-kill-a-mockingbird-2016-2.

2. Emily Rella, "By the Numbers: 'To Kill a Mockingbird,'" AOL.com, February 19, 2016, https://www.aol.com/article/2016/02/19/by-the-numbers-to-kill-a-mockingbird/21315602/?guccounter=1& guce_referrer=aHR0cHM6Ly93d3cuZ29vZ2xlLmNvbS88& guce_referrer_sig= AQAAAERnMMiDKJfjFoi1xV_21b1L1QvesoSNLV0plsLilNvM3Ts9F2k G5dCxni74h0SEQZdYAnUPXgvooPii7kBA_iIIq1V13hMngMXhWRhLT k_uScXDwea-n2k7p9WYNrWh1o- BaFTRhbat50Tt19XZz1JYA9lhTz21ByWzxpTnZduG.

3. Margalit Fox, "Michael Brown, 93, Dies; Industrial Musicals Gave Wings to 'Mockingbird,'" *New York Times*, June 29, 2014, https://www.nytimes.com/2014/06/30/arts/music/michael-brown-whose-industrial-musicals-gave-wings-to-to-kill-a-mockingbird-dies-at-93.html.

4. "Achievements," Ellafitzgerald.com, accessed March 31, 2020, http://www.ellafitzgerald.com/about/achievements.

5. Rose Heichelbech, "The Compelling Friendship between Ella Fitzgerald and Marilyn Monroe," Dustyoldthing.com, accessed March 31, 2020, https://dustyoldthing.com/ella-fitzgerald-marilyn-monroe-friendship/; Sara Kettler, "Ella Fitzgerald and Marilyn Monroe: Inside Their Surprising Friendship," Biography.com, June 24, 2019, https://www.biography.com/news/marilyn-monroe-ella-fitzgerald-friendship; Erin McCann, "How Marilyn Monroe and Ella Fitzgerald's Friendship Gave Them Both Their Careers," Ranker.com, April 26, 2019, https://www.ranker.com/list/ella-fitzgerald-marilyn-monroe-friendship-careers/erin-mccann.

6. Kettler, "Ella Fitzgerald and Marilyn Monroe."

7. McCann, "How Marilyn Monroe and Ella Fitzgerald's Friendship Gave Them Both Their Careers."

8. Lidiya K., "Ed Sheeran's Life Story: How a Bullied Ginger Boy Became Britain's Biggest Music Success," Goalcast.com, January 9, 2018, https://www.goalcast.com/2018/01/09/ed-sheeran-life-story-2/.

9. JD Knapp, "Jamie Foxx Let Ed Sheeran Crash on His Couch before the

Brit Made It Big," Variety.com, June 24, 2017, https://variety.com/2017/music/news/jamie-foxx-ed-sheeran-before-he-was-famous-graham-norton-show-1202477734/.

10. Stephen, "Ed Sheeran Albums and Songs Sales," Chartmasters.com, accessed April 5, 2020, https://chartmasters.org/2019/10/ed-sheeran-albums-and-songs-sales-2/.

11. Evan Beard, "What Billionaire Collectors Would Pay for the 'Priceless' Art in U.S. Museums," Artsy.com, April 18, 2018, https://www.artsy.net/article/artsy-editorial-billionaire-collectors-pay-priceless-art-museums.

12. David Sheward, "7 Facts about Vincent van Gogh," Biography.com, March 29, 2016, https://www.biography.com/news/vincent-van-gogh-biography-facts.

19. Personal Purpose

1. Api Podder, "How Tony Robbins Was Inspired by a Turkey to Feed Millions," Yourmarkontheworld.com, December 18, 2015, https://yourmarkontheworld.com/how-tony-robbins-was-inspired-by-a-turkey-to-feed-millions/.

2. Podder, "How Tony Robbins Was Inspired by a Turkey to Feed Millions."

3. Team Tony, "One Meal at a Time. One Billion Meals in Total," Tonyrobbins.com, accessed April 20, 2020, https://www.tonyrobbins.com/news/one-billion-meals-challenge/.

4. Biography.com Editors, "Biography of Harriet Tubman," Biography.com, February 28, 2018, https://www.biography.com/activist/harriet-tubman.

5. Kate Clifford Larson, Ph.D., "Bound for the Promised Land: Harriet Tubman, Portrait of an American Hero," Harriettubmanbiography.com, accessed April 17, 2020, http://www.harriettubmanbiography.com/harriet-tubman-myths-and-facts.html.

6. Larson, "Bound for the Promised Land: Harriet Tubman, Portrait of an American Hero."

7. Biography.com Editors, "Biography of Harriet Tubman."

8. Rosie Hopegood, "'I Was Raped and Left for Dead—My Anger Has Put 1,200 Criminals behind Bars,'" *Mirror*, August 11, 2019, https://www.mirror.co.uk/news/real-life-stories/incredible-skteches-woman-raped-choke-18856366.

9. Hopegood, "'I Was Raped and Left for Dead—My Anger Has Put 1,200 Criminals behind Bars.'"

10. Kristen Stephenson, "The World's Most Successful Forensic Artist: How Lois Gibson's Incredible Sketches Have Helped Solve Thousands of Crimes," Guinnessworldrecords.com, January 18, 2017, https://www.guinnessworldrecords.com/news/2017/1/lois-gibson-facing-crime-with-world-records-458852.

11. David Lumu, "Fifty Percent of Land Is Disputed—Uhrc Report," New Vision, May 24, 2018, https://www.newvision.co.ug/news/1478385/fifty-percent-land-disputed-uhrc-report.

12. Liam Taylor, "Out of Court: Ugandans Turn to 'Barefoot Lawyers' to Settle Land Disputes," Reuters, January 23, 2020, https://www.reuters.com/article/us-uganda-landrights-justice/out-of-court-ugandans-turn-to-barefoot-lawyers-to-settle-land-disputes-idUSKBN1ZM19Y.

13. "Ugandan Man Becomes a Lawyer to Win Family Land Back," April 3, 2019, https://www.bbc.com/news/world-africa-47801008.

14. "Ugandan Man Becomes a Lawyer to Win Family Land Back."

15. Water.org Editors, "A Women's Crisis," Water.org, accessed April 22, 2020, https://water.org/our-impact/water-crisis/womens-crisis/; Water.org Editors, "The Water Crisis," Water.org, accessed April 22, 2020, https://water.org/our-impact/water-crisis/.

20. Unexpected Purpose

1. Roger Maynard, "Australia Mourns 'Angel of the Gap' Don Ritchie, the Man Who Talked 160 Out of Suicide," *Independent*, May 16, 2012, https://www.independent.co.uk/news/people/news/australia-mourns-angel-of-the-gap-don-ritchie-the-man-who-talked-160-out-of-suicide-7754339.html.

2. Talia Ralph, "Don Ritchie, an Australian Man Who Talked Over 160 People Out Suicide, Dead at 85," The World, May 14, 2012, https://www.pri.org/stories/2012-05-14/don-ritchie-australian-man-who-talked-over-160-people-out-suicide-dead-85.

3. Ralph, "Don Ritchie."

4. Nobuki Sugihara, "My Father, the Quiet Hero: How Japan's Schindler Saved 6,000 Jews," *Guardian*, January 4, 2020, https://www.theguardian.com/world/2020/jan/04/chiune-sugihara-my-father-japanese-schindler-saved-6000-jews-lithuania.

5. Cnaan Liphshiz, "Holocaust Hero Chiune Sugihara's Son Sets Record

Straight on His Father's Story," Times of Israel, May 23, 2019, https://www.timesofisrael.com/holocaust-hero-chiune-sugiharas-son-sets-record-straight-on-his-fathers-story/.

6. Tricia Seaman with Diane Nichols, *God Gave Me You: A True Story of Love, Loss, and a Heaven-Sent Miracle* (New York: Howard Books, 2016).

7. Bob Goff, *Everybody Always: Becoming Love in a World Full of Setbacks and Difficult People* (Nashville: Nelson Books, 2018).

8. Jennie Key, "Christmas Comes Early to Colerain Twp. Tot Suffering with Brain Cancer," *Cincinnati Enquirer*, September 19, 2018, https://www.cincinnati.com/story/news/local/colerain/2018/09/19/christmas-comes-early-colerain-twp-tot-suffering-brain-cancer/1299689002/.

9. Bob D'Angelo, "Cancer-Stricken Toddler Brody Allen, Who Got an Early Christmas, Dies," *Dayton Daily News*, October 20, 2018, https://www.daytondailynews.com/news/cancer-stricken-toddler-brody-allen-who-got-early-christmas-dies/LJsCHJrqY359Q18d1as6CI/.

21. Purpose at Work

1. History.com Editors, "Great Depression History," History.com, accessed April 26, 2020, https://www.history.com/topics/great-depression/great-depression-history.

2. Natalie Colarossi, "25 Vintage Photos Show How Desperate and Desolate America Looked during the Great Depression, the Last Time the Unemployment Rate Was as High as It Is Today," Insider.com, May 11, 2020, https://www.insider.com/great-depression-photos-of-america-unemployment-2020-5.

3. Anupam Pant, "The Role of Wind in a Tree's Life," Awesome Science, Accessed March 2020, http://awesci.com/the-role-of-wind-in-a-trees-life/.

22. Do It Responsibly

1. Ted Allrich, "How Much Money Is Enough?," Nasdaq.com, AUG 27, 2010, https://www.nasdaq.com/articles/how-much-money-enough-2010-08-27.

23. Do It Consistently

1. Kashmira Gander, "Blood Donor, 81, Who Saved 2.4 Million Babies Offers Up 'Golden Arm' for the Final Time," *Newsweek*, May 11, 2018, https://www.newsweek.com/blood-donor-james-harrison-saved-24million-babies-golden-arm-final-time-921433.
2. "He Donated Blood Every Week for 60 Years and Saved the Lives of 2.4 Million Babies," News Channel 2 WKTV, May 11, 2018, https://www.wktv.com/templates/AMP?contentID=482383831.
3. Amy B. Wang, "For Six Decades, 'the Man with the Golden Arm' Donated Blood—and Saved 2.4 Million Babies," *Chicago Tribune*, May 12, 2018, https://www.chicagotribune.com/nation-world/ct-blood-donor-james-harrison-saved-babies-20180512-story.html.

24. Do It Habitually

1. David T. Neal, Wendy Wood, and Jeffrey M. Quinn, "Habits—A Repeat Performance," *Current Directions in Psychological Science* 15, no. 4 (2006), https://dornsife.usc.edu/assets/sites/545/docs/Wendy_Wood_Research_Articles/Habits/Neal.Wood.Quinn.2006_Habits_a_repeat_performance.pdf.
2. Charles Duhigg, *The Power of Habit: Why We Do What We Do in Life and Business*, (New York: Random House, 2012).
3. Jordan Crook, "Cycflix Lets You Watch Netflix, but Only If You Keep Up the Pace," TechCrunch, July 27, 2017, https://techcrunch.com/2017/07/27/cycflix-lets-you-watch-netflix-but-only-if-you-keep-up-the-pace/?guccounter=1&guce_referrer=aHR0cHM6Ly93d3cuZ29vZ2xlLmNvbS8&guce_referrer_sig=AQAAALuxwuUQVrXQ98MS4uh0zdJpEMCnGNZ-l4oOiWWNVxgG3S2ZNlGdq1dChm8IBGHh43OC1tdc0pD8C17RYP0u bi5CQzLGc8lMSyZ6e88MX_awH7tuqG072do_RNX9crz_dABlAlKZQnJb0SDxBEYAHxBnSE1aBc87BcWU2RC-v01w.
4. James Clear, *Atomic Habits: An Easy & Proven Way to Build Good Habits & Break Bad Ones*, (New York: Avery, 2018).

25. Do It Despite the Difficulties

1. Joseph Bentley, "Success Story: Keith Jarrett and the 'Unplayable' Piano," TamingWickedProblems.com, October 2, 2017, http://tamingwickedproblems.com/success-story-keith-jarrett-and-the-unplayable-piano/.
2. Bill Janovitz, "The 40th Anniversary of Keith Jarrett's Legendary 'Köln Concert,'" *Observer*, March 12, 2015,https://observer.com/2015/03/the-40th-anniversary-of-keith-jarretts-legendary-koln-concert/.
3. NPR/TED staff, "Tim Harford: How Can Chaos Lead to Creative Break-throughs?," TED Radio Hour, NPR, May 10, 2019, https://www.npr.org/2019/05/10/719557642/tim-harford-how-can-chaos-lead-to-creative-breakthroughs.

26. Do What You Can

1. Genevieve Shaw Brown, "Man's T-Shirt Plea for Kidney Leads to Live Organ Donor Match," ABC News, December 22, 2017, https://abcnews.go.com/Lifestyle/mans-shirt-plea-kidney-leads-live-organ-donor/story?id=51862120.
2. "Dying New Jersey Dad Gets Kidney Transplant after Disney Photo Goes Viral," ABC News, January 26, 2018, https://abc7ny.com/disney-kidney-world-donor/2992860/.

27. Do It with Determination

1. Marvin Olasky, "Theodore Roosevelt Found God's Faithfulness after Disaster," *World Magazine*, February 13, 1999, https://world.wng.org/1999/02/healing_the_heart.
2. "'The Light Has Gone Out of My Life'—Teddy Roosevelt's Diary Entry on the Day Both His Wife and Mother Died," Vintage News Daily, August 28, 2019, https://vintagenewsdaily.com/the-light-has-gone-out-of-my-life-teddy-roosevelts-diary-entry-on-the-day-both-his-wife-and-mother-died-1884/.
3. Aine Cain, "US President Theodore Roosevelt Once Delivered an 84-Minute Speech after Getting Shot in the Chest," *Business Insider*, June 21, 2017, https://www.businessinsider.com/teddy-roosevelt-assassination-attempt-2017-6.

28. Do It Until

1. Carole Cadwalladr, "Endurance Swimmer Diana Nyad: 'It's about Having a Steel-Trap Mind,'" *Guardian*, July 10, 2016, https://www. theguardian.com/lifeandstyle/2016/jul/10/endurance-swimmer-diana-nyad-its-about-steel-trap-mind.
2. Tom Brown, "American Diana Nyad Gives Up Latest Cuba-U.S. Swim Attempt," Reuters, August 21, 2012, https://www.reuters.com/article/us-cuba-swim/american-diana-nyad-gives-up-latest-cuba-u-s-swim-attempt-idUSBRE87K0J120120821.
3. Mike Braun, "Florida Kayakers Help Swimmer Nyad Reach Historic Goal," *USA Today*, September 5, 2013, https://www.usatoday.com/story/news/nation/2013/09/05/diana-nyad-support-crew/2772667/.

30. You Get to Choose

1. The Editors of Encyclopaedia Britannica, "Viktor Frankl," *Encyclopaedia Britannica*, accessed March 20, 2020, https://www.britannica.com/biography/Viktor-Frankl.
2. Viktor Frankl, *Man's Search for Meaning* (Boston: Beacon Press, 1959).

31. Seize the Day

1. *Dead Poet's Society*, directed by Peter Weir, written by Tom Schulman (Burbank: Touchstone Pictures, 1989).
2. David Goggins, *Can't Hurt Me: Master Your Mind and Defy the Odds*, (Austin: Lioncrest Publishing, 2018).

32. Don't Let Ugly Stop You

1. Stephen Miller, "Mike Yurosek, 82, Farmer Who Invented Baby Carrots," *The New York Sun*, June 24, 2005, https://www.nysun.com/obituaries/mike-yurosek-82-farmer-who-invented-baby-carrots/16046/.
2. The Origin and Evolution of Baby Carrots, accessed April 12, 2020, http://www.carrotmuseum.co.uk/babycarrot.html.

33. There's Still Time

1. "Oldest College Grad," Passiton.com, accessed March 20, 2020, https://www.passiton.com/inspirational-sayings-billboards/28-live-life.
2. "Nola Ochs . . . at 95, Not Just Another College Graduate!," Mybestyears.com, accessed March 20, 2020, http://www.mybestyears.com/InterviewSpotlights/OCHSNola042707.html.
3. Kara Goldfarb, "He Was the Oldest Man to Climb Mount Everest—10 Years Later He Beat His Own Record," Allthatsinteresting.com, May 14, 2018, https://allthatsinteresting.com/yuichiro-miura.

35. What If It's True?

1. Blaise Pascal, *Pensées*, (New York: Penguin Classics, 1995).
2. Bertrand Russell, *The Autobiography of Bertrand Russell*, (New York: Routledge, 2000).
3. John 10:10, Biblica, *The Holy Bible*, New International Version (NIV), 2011, https://www.biblegateway.com/passage/?search=John+10%3A10&version=NIV.

36. This Is All We Can Do

1. Warren Boroson, "A Memorable Story from WW2," *Jewish Standard*, January 6, 2014, https://jewishstandard.timesofisrael.com/a-memorable-story-from-ww2-2/.

37. Marathon of Hope

1. "It's Got to Keep Going without Me," Terryfox.org, accessed March 20, 2020, https://terryfox.org/terrys-story/marathon-of-hope/.
2. Jane Stevenson, "Running with Terry Fox: Adidas Releases Marathon of Hope Anniversary Shoe," *Toronto Sun*, May 19, 2020, https://torontosun.com/life/fashion-beauty/running-with-terry-fox-adidas-releases-marathon-of-hope-anniversary-shoe.
3. Gord Noble, "Terry Fox's Marathon of Hope Driver and Best Buddy Visits Penticton Terry Fox Run," Penticton Now, September 16, 2019,

https://www.pentictonnow.com/watercooler/news/news/Penticton/Terry_Fox_s_Marathon_of_Hope_driver_and_best_buddy_vi sits_Penticton_Terry_Fox_Run/.

4. Sean Mitton, "Isadore Sharp Recalls Terry Fox Luncheon and the Paper-clip," CEN Newsletters, accessed March 21, 2020, http://www.canadianexpatnetwork.com/public/606.cfm.

5. Jeremy Freeborn, "Rick Hansen," *Canadian Encyclopedia*, March 24, 2008, https://www.thecanadianencyclopedia.ca/en/article/rick-hansen.

6. John Brant, "Following Terry Fox," *Runners World*, January 7, 2016, https://www.runnersworld.com/runners-stories/a20783824/terry-foxs-marathon-of-hope/.

7. "Terry Fox Run – Sunday, September 15, 2019 Old Port of Montreal," *The Montrealer*, September 10, 2019, https://themontrealeronline.com/2019/09/terry-fox-run-sunday-september-15-2019-old-port-of-montreal/.

8. Tim Huebsch, "The Annual Terry Fox Run Was First Held 35 Years Ago Today," *Running*, September 13, 2016, https://runningmagazine.ca/sections/runs-races/the-annual-terry-fox-run-was-first-held-35-years-ago-today/.

9. Douglas Finley, "Terry Fox's Transformational Run," Podium Runner, April 10, 2020, https://www.podiumrunner.com/culture/terry-foxs-transformational-run/.

10. Michael LoRé, "Dick Traum Turns Tragedy of Losing Leg into Inspira-tion for Others," Culture Trip, February 22, 2017, https://theculturetrip.com/north-america/usa/new-york/articles/dick-traum-turns-tragedy-of-losing-leg-into-inspiration-for-others/.

11. Amy Judd, "A Look at the Changes in Cancer Research Since Terry Fox Was Diagnosed in 1977," Global News, September 13, 2013, https://globalnews.ca/news/840439/a-look-at-the-changes-in-cancer-research-since-terry-fox-was-diagnosed-in-1977/.

12. Josh K. Elliott, "Terry Fox Superfan, 7, Asking for Cancer Donations Instead of Candy at Halloween," Global News, October 30, 2019, https://globalnews.ca/news/6101948/terry-fox-run-costume-halloween/.

13. Amy Borkowski, "A True Canadian Hero," Wattpad.com, accessed April 11, 2020, https://www.wattpad.com/810693425-terry-fox-a-true-canadian-hero-biography.

38. Will This Work?

1. "Never Give In, Never, Never, Never, 1941," Nationalchurchillmuseum.org, accessed April 17, 2020, https://www.nationalchurchillmuseum.org/never-give-in-never-never-never.html.

CONNECT WITH KEVIN

If you'd like to connect with Kevin, he'd love to hear from you. You can reach him at:

KevinJohnDelaney@gmail.com

You can also stay connected by visiting or subscribing to Kevin's website and blog:

KevinJohnDelaney.com

Kevin frequently delivers workshops and speaks to audiences. If you are interested in having Kevin speak at an event, please visit Kevin's website for information.

Made in the USA
Coppell, TX
01 December 2020